Adam Badeau

**Aristocracy in England**

Adam Badeau

**Aristocracy in England**

ISBN/EAN: 9783744715812

Printed in Europe, USA, Canada, Australia, Japan

Cover: Foto ©Suzi / pixelio.de

More available books at **www.hansebooks.com**

# ARISTOCRACY IN ENGLAND

By ADAM BADEAU
AUTHOR OF "MILITARY HISTORY OF ULYSSES S. GRANT" AND
"CONSPIRACY: A CUBAN ROMANCE"

NEW YORK
HARPER & BROTHERS, FRANKLIN SQUARE
1886

# CONTENTS.

| No. | | Page |
|---|---|---|
| | INTRODUCTION | 5 |
| I. | The Queen | 7 |
| II. | At Court | 17 |
| III. | Rank and Title | 29 |
| IV. | Primogeniture | 42 |
| V. | Precedence | 52 |
| VI. | The Prince of Wales | 61 |
| VII. | Americans at Court | 71 |
| VIII. | The Crown in Politics | 83 |
| IX. | The Personal Character of the Queen | 94 |
| X. | Precedence in the Servants' Hall | 103 |
| XI. | The House of Lords | 113 |
| XII. | The Princess of Wales | 125 |
| XIII. | American Ministers | 135 |
| XIV. | Manners | 146 |
| XV. | Caste | 155 |
| XVI. | Illegitimacy | 165 |
| XVII. | Servants in the Country | 173 |
| XVIII. | Servants in Town | 183 |
| XIX. | A Nobleman Indeed | 193 |

| No. | Page |
|---|---|
| XX. Spiritual Peers | 201 |
| XXI. The Pomps and Vanities of the Church | 208 |
| XXII. Church and State | 214 |
| XXIII. The House of Commons | 222 |
| XXIV. The Land | 230 |
| XXV. Entail | 238 |
| XXVI. Sport | 246 |
| XXVII. The Accessions | 256 |
| XXVIII. Literature and the Lords | 264 |
| XXIX. The London Season | 272 |
| XXX. Aristocratic Influence | 281 |
| Gladstone—The Iconoclast | 289 |

# INTRODUCTION.

The one thing which more than any other, for an American, distinguishes English life and civilization from his own is—Aristocracy. Even Europeans find the characteristics of the British people more affected by caste than is the case with the most enlightened races of the Continent, while the existence and influence of the institution are to a democrat, fresh from the equality and uniformity of social and political life in the New World, matter of unceasing marvel. After twelve years spent in England, the spectacle was to me as remarkable as ever, and it remains my deliberate opinion that the relations of the aristocracy with the Court, the Government and politics, with the Church, with literature, the army and navy—even with trade and manufactures, and certainly with agriculture and the land, with the dependent classes and the very poor—constitute the pivot on which all English life revolves, the feature which is most marked in the national character and polity; the explanation of what is most peculiar, the charm of what is most attractive, and the root of what is most repelling; the strength of what is greatest in the past or firmest in the present, as well as the weakness and danger of whatever is most threatened now, or most certainly doomed in the future.

With this belief I propose to give some account of the English aristocracy, as I had the opportunity of seeing and studying it between the years 1869 and 1881. My chapters are not designed to form the groundwork of an attack nor to hold up even the excellent points of an aristocracy for the imitation of republicans; they are intended neither for an exhaustive treatise nor a political disquisition; but to set forth what I have myself seen and known; to tell what struck me as most curious or interesting; to offer a picture of an institution which has had an immense influence on the whole modern world, but which, with all its glories, its pomp and power, its fascinations and its faults, its vices and its virtues, is destined soon to take a place by the side of the Roman Empire and the Venetian oligarchy. It may be well to portray some of its more salient features before the stately but time-worn fabric falls.

# ARISTOCRACY IN ENGLAND.

## I.

### THE QUEEN.

The Queen is the head of the aristocracy. With many of its members, in one way or another, she is allied. A large number of those of ancient lineage quarter the royal arms, very many, it is true, with the bar sinister; but probably a third of the great families of the realm can trace their descent, legitimately or illegitimately, from a former sovereign. In official documents the monarch styles every peer above the rank of baron, "cousin," and the Queen's own children sit in the House of Lords. The Duke of Wellington once refused to apologize to a brother of George IV. for words spoken in that assembly, although the King demanded it, for "there," he said, "we are all peers."

Not a few of the aristocracy are literally cousins of the present Queen. The last King, her uncle, ennobled seven of his illegitimate children, while two others married peers. One of these first cousins was for a long time Her Majesty's housekeeper, another her naval aid-de-camp. They are proud of the kinship, too, and sport the royal liveries.

There are connections, however, that Victoria does not recognize. The line seems to be drawn at the descendants of sovereigns. One of the family habitually visits German watering-places with a lady who is not his wife, and duchesses dine with her because of her relations with royalty; but the sullied gentlewoman never went to Windsor. Her Majesty countenances no such conduct in subjects, of whatever degree. It is needless to say that her own life has been a model of purity.

The only marriage with one of her subjects which the Queen has authorized is that of her daughter, the Princess Louise, with the Marquis of Lorne, eldest son of the Duke of Argyll. This was the first that had been sanctioned by both Crown and Church since James II. married the daughter of Clarendon. Two of the sons of George II., it is true, married into the aristocracy, but the wife was never allowed the precedence of a sovereign's child, and since the time of the Duchess of Cumberland, in 1771, a marriage of one of the royal family has been invalid without the permission of the Crown. The Duke of Sussex, one of the Queen's uncles, was married to the daughter of an earl, who never bore her husband's title, or was received at court; and after that lady's death, he contracted a morganatic marriage, which also gave his wife no rank nor precedence. Yet both were women of unblemished virtue, and the second was made a duchess, though not with her husband's title; the Queen visited her, and the Prince of Wales attended her funeral. She simply could not be admitted to that exalted sphere, reserved for royalty alone, "unmixed with baser matter."

The Queen, however, not only permitted, but made, the marriage of the Princess Louise. If the story universally current is true, the royal maiden returned the regard of her brother's tutor, who had dared to cast his eyes so high, and there was danger of a contingency entirely contrary to royal etiquette, of a marriage beyond even the morganatic sphere. To prevent a catastrophe so appalling, a place in the Church was given to the tutor, which separated him from the palace, and the hand of the Princess was offered to several of the young nobility in turn, but the distinction was declined, until finally Lord Lorne consented to enter the royal family. The Queen, however, had not foreseen the humiliations which such a connection would impose. When the Duke of Argyll went to pay his first visit at Windsor after the engagement of his son, he ventured to kiss the lady who was about to become his daughter. One who was present assured me that the Queen reddened and drew back with indignation at the liberty.

Yet Her Majesty sanctioned the marriage of the Princess Helena with a prince who already had a morganatic wife, and she has just given the youngest of her daughters to another, supposed by royalty to be so far beneath its sphere that the imperial family of Germany refused to be present at the ceremony. The connections of the Queen, indeed, range to the very extremities of the (royal) social scale. One of her children is married to the son of the greatest of living potentates, another to the daughter of a Czar, while a third accepted a commoner, the mere heir to a dukedom; and the sister of her favorite son-in-law, a Princess of Sleswig-Holstein, the aunt of Her Majesty's grandchildren, is absolutely married to a physician, and what is worse, with Her Majesty's approval. I knew a doctor's wife in England whom that Princess visited, and who evidently felt that they both belonged to the profession. Whether she was connected with royalty, or royalty with physic and therefore with her, I could not tell, but she always put on airs when she talked of the Princess.

These social *faux pas* of the Queen she seems at other times inclined to atone for by a rigorous conformity to etiquette. She received the Shah of Persia as a brother monarch, met him at the threshold of Windsor, and offered her cheek to be kissed by the barbarian because he was a reigning sovereign, though she had shuddered to see her daughter saluted by the MacCallum More. Perhaps she thought the dusky embrace might wipe out the memory of the *mésalliance*. Then, too, when the late Emperor of the French had reached the purple by perfidy and fraud, she buckled the Garter on the adventurer's knee, although years before she had refused him admission to her court. She even kept up the intimacy after he had fallen. Napoleon III. was a frequent visitor at Buckingham Palace during his exile, and the Empress is perhaps the one woman whom the Queen of England has ever regarded with the friendship bestowed on equals. With no other crowned head has she been on similar terms. Yet, however dignified the behavior of Eugénie may have been in later days, the career of Mlle. de Montijo would certainly have excluded her from the presence of the English Queen. The future sovereign was visiting in the family of a lady whom I know, when the Emperor's passion became evident; and the astute hostess has told me of the advice she thought it necessary to give her guest. "If you never see him alone," she said, "you will certainly become an empress." The Spanish beauty heeded the sagacious counsel, and mounted the imperial throne. Once a bishop always a bishop, and having worn a crown the parvenu potentates could not be divested of the divinity that doth hedge even upstart kings and successful usurpers, though the French people had dismissed and dethroned them. At least the superstition lingers in royal minds.

Misfortune, however, in some eyes atones for crimes, and the fact that they were fallen gave these ephemeral royalties, perhaps, a claim upon their more fortunate sister. The Queen, indeed, has always shown undiminished deference to the members of dethroned dynasties. The King of Hanover received royal honors in England after his crown was snatched from him by the remorseless Bismarck, and at his death he enjoyed the distinction of a royal funeral. So, too, the Orleans princes during their long exile were always recognized as royal. They, however, were relatives, and entitled to consideration on that score.

But the principle was carried to the extreme in the case of the son of Theodore, His late Majesty of Abyssinia. The British arms had overturned that sable sovereign, who died in defence of his kingdom, and his son became a prisoner and a pensioner in England. I was once at a gathering of the clans in the neighborhood of Balmoral, at which Prince Leopold was present and the Prime Minister of the day. They came together, and in the same carriage was the African Prince of the blood. He looked to me like any little negro boy of nine or ten; but he had his gentlemen in waiting, he took precedence of the Prime Minister, and he stood on the red carpet reserved for royalty alone.

The Queen still exacts for herself the punctilio of former centuries. Men and women of the highest rank kneel to her to-day; Cabinet Ministers kiss her hand. She refuses to receive any personal service from a menial, except at table. She never opens a door or directs a letter. Dukes and duchesses cloak her in public, and commoners become "Honorable" for life because they have waited on Her Majesty. At a garden party I have seen a duchess walking behind her to carry a bouquet, or standing at the entrance of a tent while her mistress went within to rest or refresh herself. The sovereign's own daughters arrange her robes when she opens Parliament; the Prince of Wales pays homage as a subject on the same occasion; her children must be presented at court upon their marriage. In the early part of her reign she was visiting Louis Philippe, then King of the French, at his Château d'Eu, and one day asked for a glass of water. It was handed her by a servant, but Her Majesty declined to receive it; whereupon the King directed one of his own sons to offer the goblet, which then was graciously accepted.

The ladies and gentlemen in waiting are not expected to sit in the presence of royalty, and countesses and marchionesses get themselves larger shoes because they must stand so long. I knew a personal attendant of the Queen who acted as secretary, a woman of very high rank, and as old as Her Majesty, who often, after writing till she was exhausted, asked permission to finish on her knees.

Those who have the honor of dining at Windsor are shown after dinner into a long gallery where there are no seats, and perforce they stand till Her Majesty is ready to retire. Then I have seen two duchesses approach and throw a shawl across the shoulders of the Queen, literally acting as mistresses of the robes.

Yet the countesses and duchesses are seldom willing to surrender their posts. There seems a fascination about the life, in spite of its irksomeness. Many of the same lords and ladies have been in attendance on the Queen for years, and some of them certainly entertain a profound affection for Her Majesty. Indeed, although at drawing-rooms and on the rare occasions when the Queen is seen in public her demeanor is reserved and her expression almost stern, all this is changed with individuals. The plain and stout lady, rather dowdily dressed, becomes gracious and winning in the last degree. Her whole face is lighted with the desire to please and the certainty that she succeeds. There is something more than suave or urbane in both smile and bearing, something not exactly of condescension, for the consciousness of superiority is necessary for this, and it is the consciousness only of her grandeur, not of your inferiority, that she feels and makes you feel—a triumph of manner worthy of the greatest of actresses, or of a queen.

I can speak without prejudice or partiality, for the only opportunity I have had of conversing with Her Majesty was when I thought I had been treated with discourtesy; but even then the sweetness of her behavior overcame my soreness and subdued my not unnatural resentment. Her first utterance was to thank me for a book I had sent her seven years before, and which had been acknowledged at the time, and every syllable she spoke was intended to give me pleasure. The acts of the Queen may sometimes seem ungracious, her action, never, I am told.

I was once strongly reminded of the great geniuses of the stage by the mien and deportment of the Majesty of England. It was at the opening of the Albert Hall. The building was crowded to its utmost, and the Queen walked down the vast amphitheatre to what may be called the stage, preceded and followed by great dignitaries and accompanied by the Prince and Princess of Wales. When she turned to face the multitude eight thousand people were standing in her honor, and the cheers were deafening. And then there came across her features an expression which it is hardly possible to describe; her face fairly shone with gratification at the loyalty of her people and motherly affection for them in return. She courtesied again and again, lower and lower, exactly like a great actress playing a queen who had been called out to receive the plaudits of her audience. But of all the famous mistresses of the stage that I have seen, the women of genius who enraptured nations, none ever surpassed in grace or dignity, at the proudest moments of her mimicry, this real sovereign acknowledging absolute homage.

## II.

### AT COURT.

The intercourse of a British subject of the upper classes with the sovereign usually begins with a presentation at court; but there are still houses where the Queen visits personally an old or invalid friend, and the children may thus be earlier brought into the presence of royalty. After the Thanksgiving for the recovery of the Prince of Wales there was much unfavorable comment because Her Majesty had appeared at Saint Paul's in bonnet and shawl, although peers and members of the House of Commons were compelled to wear levee dress. Former sovereigns on similar occasions had worn their robes and crowns, and the loyal throng had been greatly disappointed at not beholding their Queen in "all her proud attire." The next day Her Majesty paid a visit to the mother of a duke who had been unable to leave her couch for years. Notice as usual was given in advance, the house was prepared, the red carpet laid, the gentlemen of the family were in evening dress, and the Queen was received with the proper etiquette. During her stay she was petting a little boy some five or six years old, when the urchin, who had heard the talk about Saint Paul's, cried out, to the horror of the family: "Are you the Queen? Why didn't you wear your crown?" But only the scions of illustrious houses enjoy such opportunities of direct and early communication with royalty. Young ladies of quality are usually presented to Her Majesty upon their entrance into society, and the men as they emerge from hobble-de-hoy-hood or the university.

The first day I spent in London I went to a levee. It was held by the Prince of Wales, and only men attended. I was then a Secretary of Legation, so that I had what are called the *entrées*, and enjoyed peculiar opportunities for watching the spectacle. The Prince was standing with his attendants in the throne-room when the diplomatists entered in the order of their rank, and those of the same rank according to the seniority of their standing at the English court. This point of precedence was thought of sufficient importance to be established at the Congress of Vienna, and the representatives of the United States conform to the rule. Each ambassador or minister is followed by the members of his embassy or legation, who have no place of their own; they are simply the suite of their chief.

The Prince was at the head of the room facing

the entrance; on his left were his brothers and the other men of the royal family, all arranged punctiliously according to their degree; then came the Government of the day; on the right were the courtiers in attendance, the whole forming a semicircle, which extended to the doors for entrance and exit on the opposite side of the room. Each person coming to court brings a card, with his name or title written out in full; this is given up at the door and passed along to the Lord Chamberlain, who stands next to the Prince and reads the card aloud. A profound bow is all the obeisance required from men. If the Prince, however, knows the visitor well or wishes to do him especial honor, he extends his hand, which can only be taken by an ungloved hand in return, so that "No gloves at court" is a peremptory etiquette, at least for the right hand. After a reverence to each of the royal personages, the members of the diplomatic corps take up their positions immediately opposite the Prince and his surroundings, thus forming a narrow lane, through which all after comers must pass, for the diplomatists constitute a part of the court, and must remain until royalty leaves the room.

All others, except a very few great personages who have the *entrées*, pass directly through the lane of dignitaries and into an anteroom, so that for them the ceremony lasts but a moment; but the procession continues, sometimes for hours, and as every one but an American is in some showy dress, the effect to an unaccustomed eye is decidedly imposing. I was particularly struck at my first levee with the manly beauty of the young aristocrats. I was not then familiar with the ruddy complexions and brown or golden hair, the superb forms and graceful bearing that abundant exercise and the peculiar climate combine to give the British youth of the higher class. Arrayed in Highland kilt or military scarlet, or even in the plainer breeches and laced coat of the modern courtier, they passed along, by far the handsomest set of men I had ever seen.

I must say, however, that the show outside was finer still. The huge footmen were sometimes smarter than their masters in looks as well as clothes, for the court liveries are often the dress worn by the nobility in former times, while the lackeys themselves are selected for their height and the size of their calves. I know a duchess who, whenever she hires a footman, makes him get into breeches and march up and down in her dining-room till she can decide whether his shape and his walk are what her dignity requires.

A drawing-room is held by the Queen, or on rare occasions by the Princess of Wales. It is intended only for ladies, and the announcement is made in the public prints that "noblemen and gentlemen are not expected to present themselves unless in attendance on the ladies of their families." The Queen is easily fatigued, and prefers as much as possible to limit the number of her faithful subjects on these occasions. But as everybody of consequence who is in London is supposed to go to court once a year, and as no one is invited to the Queen's balls or concerts who has not first attended a levee or drawing-room, the crowd is often very great.

The names of those not previously presented must be sent in "two clear days" in advance, as well as the names of those who present them; and it does not follow, as a matter of course, that every name is accepted. Any known immorality in a woman is fatal, no matter what her rank. On this point Her Majesty is immutable. No woman who has deserted her husband for another man, and none who has lived with a man without marriage, can ever be presented to the English Queen. If the stigma is discovered too late, a notice is inserted in the newspapers that the presentation has been cancelled. This occurred some years ago in the case of a woman of title, wife of a member of the Government. But, usually, ladies of sullied reputations are aware of Her Majesty's rule, and take care not to risk consequences so disagreeable.

Dress, however, deters quite as many as character. The regulations are as rigid on one point as the other. The oldest dowager must bare her withered arms and neck before presenting herself in the august presence, or, in order to appear with sufficient protection, a medical certificate is indispensable. Then the train must be three yards long, and the position of the feathers that must be worn is a matter of supreme importance. The Queen directs that the feathers shall be placed at the back of the head, but they must be high enough to be visible to Her Majesty when the lady enters the room. Women of rank have been turned away for neglecting some of these rules.

Court mourning, too, is a subject for the most serious consideration. The number of days it must be worn, the depth of the sorrow it indicates, the colors of the fans and the shoes, are all prescribed; and the presence-chamber of Her Majesty after a person of royal rank in Siam or Brazil has gone to receive his deserts in some other world, is lugubrious in the last degree. A black drawing-room, as it is called, would be unendurable were it not that all is so manifestly matter of form. The grief that court ladies feel on the death of the uncle of the Czar, or of some petty cousin of the Queen, whom even Her Majesty has seldom seen, can hardly be very profound. Besides, if the mourning lasts more than ten days, they are generally allowed to mitigate its sombreness with purple or red, and though their clothes must be as black as the court circular requires, they may go to as many balls as they please.

There is a long and tedious time to be endured by those whom loyalty takes to court. At both levee and drawing-room the visitors must pass through different apartments, to which they are admitted in sections; ropes are drawn across these rooms to prevent the aristocrats behind from pushing forward too eagerly, and the enclosures thus formed are properly enough called "pens." This device, however, does not prevent great crowding and sometimes flagrant ill-breeding in the "highest society of Europe." The daughter of an earl told me she had often known ladies stick pins into the bare arms of those in front to make them move out of the way; and in the rush after the ropes are withdrawn, I have twice had my epaulettes torn from my shoulders. If this should occur to an Englishman at the White House what lectures we should receive on the manners of a democracy!

The Queen, as I have said, is anxious to restrict the number of those who pay their homage. The members of the Government, however, are expected to be present whenever the sovereign holds her court, and until recently their wives as well were always in attendance, and sometimes they pretended to find the obligation irksome. But not long ago these ladies were informed that Her Majesty did not desire their company at more than a single drawing-room in a season, and they took the notification in very high dudgeon. But there was no recourse.

Indeed, when there are more than two unmarried daughters in a family, the Queen's most formal invitations expressly exclude a third. "The Ladies Guelph (2)," or "The Misses Plantagenet (2)" is the form in which the royal courtesy is extended. This limitation appears even on the cards addressed to ambassadors and the representatives of sovereign States, who are thus warned not to encroach with their whole families at once on the palatial hospitalities of England.

This cautionary notice, however, is issued only for balls and other entertainments to which the guests are specially invited. A "court" is an occasion when individuals of rank pay their respects to a royal personage, usually without actual invitation. The Lord Chamberlain makes it known that a levee or drawing-room will be held, and any whose rank entitles them are at liberty to present themselves. The diplomatic corps, as a matter of course, attend; it is, indeed, considered a discourtesy if they are absent without good cause.

But the chiefs of the corps in England not long ago received an intimation that their secretaries and attachés were not expected to be present at drawing-rooms. Now, in such matters the Queen can, of course, command her own subjects, and she certainly ought to have the right to regulate her own court; but there are no more sensitive beings on earth than diplomatic representatives away from home. They assume that all the dignity of their country is concentrated in their proper persons. The question where and how to place them arises at every ceremony, and is a constant occasion of irritation and discord. They are never satisfied, no matter what is done for them; they are exacting, proud, punctilious, and often put aside politeness for precedence and courtesy for form. Their prerogatives, they say, are matters not of privilege but of international law. I have seen them commit outrages upon good manners that the roughest American would disdain to perpetrate—thrust ladies back to take precedence of them, or leave a dinner-table because of the place to which they were assigned.

So, of course, the diplomatists resented the attempt to prohibit their suites from attending court. One ambassador declared that he represented the person of his sovereign, and that Her Majesty had no right to dictate the degree of state or the retinue with which he should present himself as his master's proxy. Accordingly he took a whole carriage-load of secretaries with him to the drawing-room; and he was admitted. For, without a doubt, and according to all the etiquettes, no sovereign can, without offence, abridge the train of an ambassador. There have been wars for what was deemed less cause.

But the ladies are waiting all this time in the pens. The presence-chamber is arranged as for a levee, only that the Queen, and not the Prince of Wales, is at the centre of the line; next are the ladies of her family, and then the heir apparent and his brothers, or any royal strangers. Her Majesty wears a black gown and a widow's cap. Over the cap is usually placed a small diamond crown, while the ribbon of the Garter and similar orders are on her breast, as well as the Koh-i-noor and other jewels worthy of a queen. The Princess of Wales and the other princesses are in full court dress—petticoats, trains, feathers, and all. Behind them stand their attendants, "male and female," as the court circular sometimes disdainfully describes them.

When the diplomatic corps has made its reverences and taken its place, the English ladies follow, and as each enters the throne-room with her train over her arm, two gentlemen in waiting deftly seize this appendage and spread it behind her, till it hangs like a peacock's drooping tail. Then the lady, handing her card to a lord-in-waiting, passes up toward the Lord Chamberlain, and stands till he pronounces her name. Upon hearing it, she prostrates herself in front of the Queen so that one knee nearly or quite touches the floor. If it is a presentation, Her Majesty extends her hand with the back upward, and the neophyte placing her own hand transversely under that of the sovereign, raises the royal extremity to her lips. When the lady is of the rank of an earl's daughter, the Queen bends slightly forward to kiss the cheek of her subject, and the homage is complete; but there have been occasions when the novice was insufficiently instructed in advance and kissed the monarch in return, very much to the disgust of Majesty and the horror-struck amazement of the courtiers. After the obeisance to the Queen, another must be made to every one in the royal circle in turn, the depth of the courtesy being graduated according to the rank of the personage; and as the last prostration is performed and the subject rises to her natural position in life again, two other watchful lords, or gentlemen, as skilful as the first, catch up her train and throw it once more over the lady's arm, and she slowly stumbles backward out of the room, having been at court.

It took her two hours, I suppose, to dress, and she sat in evening costume two hours more in line in her carriage before she entered the palace; then she was at least an hour in the pens, and she was two minutes in the presence of royalty. Now she must probably wait an hour or more for her carriage, but she has been at court. If she is young, she has practised her obeisance for days in advance, and the backward step as well, and is delighted that at last she is in the world. If she is an aspirant after social honors, a Becky Sharp working her way upward, Thackeray has told us of her sensations. If she has gone through the ceremony forty times before, she throws herself back in her carriage and exclaims, like the cockney who had seen the Apollo Belvidere: "Thank God! That's done!"

## III.

### RANK AND TITLE.

The population of England is divided into peers and commoners. There are five hundred and eighty-nine of one class and thirty-five millions of the other. The nobility, however, was at one time even more restricted in numbers. At the close of the Wars of the Roses there were twenty-nine peers left in England, and at the death of Elizabeth, in 1603, there were still only fifty-nine. In the present year of our Lord about six hundred men, with their immediate families, constitute the aristocracy of England.

The orders of nobility are five : Dukes, marquises, earls, viscounts, and barons. In every instance the eldest son succeeds by right of birth to the rank and titles of his father; but all the children of a peer are titled, and their precedence is strictly defined. Nevertheless they are commoners in the eye of the law; their titles are by courtesy only, and in official documents the eldest son of the Duke of Argyll is described as " John Campbell, commonly called the Marquis of Lorne." I once heard a very eminent man, himself a member of the aristocracy, deride the notion that the son of an English earl was noble. "That's what they call a nobleman!" said this son and brother and uncle of earls.

The wives of peers are all peeresses, and are styled duchesses, marchionesses, countesses, viscountesses, and baronesses. There are also several peeresses in their own right, for in certain families, in default of sons, the dignity descends to daughters. Should there be more than one daughter, they are co-heirs and the title remains in abeyance until only one survives. She then becomes a peeress in her own right, and transmits the succession to her eldest son. I knew such a lady, married to a commoner, and he took her family name, so that their son, who would succeed, might inherit the greater name; for no peeress can by marriage confer any rank on an ignoble husband. He remains a commoner, and upon the death of his wife will be a commoner still, though his son becomes a peer. He is not even a dowager. The dignity of Lord Great Chamberlain is hereditary in one of these families, and sometimes descends to females. It was recently in abeyance between two old ladies who together constituted the Lord Great Chamberlain of England. They were, however, allowed to depute one individual to act for both, on certain state occasions when this important functionary attends the Queen.

Scotch and Irish peers, as such, have no admission to the House of Lords, but there are twenty-eight representative Irish peers, elected by their fellows for life, who sit in that assembly, and sixteen Scotch lords, elected for a single Parliament. Very many of the nobility of Scotland and Ireland, however, are also peers of the United Kingdom, and therefore members, in their own right, of the House of Lords. Altogether there are about one hundred and forty peers without seats in the Upper Chamber. In all other respects their rights and privileges are the same as those of other peers of the same degree. Yet their dignity is less regarded. A prominent commoner once sought permission of one of the Georges to ride in a precinct of St. James's Park reserved for the royal family and the court. "No, indeed," said the King; "I will make him an Irish peer, but I won't let him ride in St. James's Park."

Two archbishops and twenty-three bishops have seats in the House of Lords, but their titles are not hereditary, and their wives have neither rank nor precedence. The Archbishop of Canterbury goes before dukes, and next after the royal family, but his wife is plain Mrs. Smith or Jones, and follows every woman who has rank of her own in the kingdom. The spiritual lords can hardly be said to belong to the aristocracy, though you would never suspect it from their bearing. They sit in its chambers and are reckoned in its degrees, but their blood is not ennobled.

Of the present peerage only about two hundred families have been noble for more than a century. At the accession of George III., in 1760, the House of Lords numbered 175 members; all the others have been created since, most of them for services to their party or the Prime Minister of the day. Pitt created fifty peers in five years, and during the seventeen years of his administration he thus rewarded 150 of his followers. That it is the minister who really confers the dignity is shown by the habit of the English writers, who no longer speak of the Queen as creating a peer, but always attribute the act to the Premier. Formerly, of course, this was the sovereign's faculty, but the power of the Crown, in this as in other matters, has passed to its nominal servants. During the twelve years that I spent in England Lord Beaconsfield and Mr. Gladstone together made sixty-one English noblemen. Of these, twenty-seven were promoted from a lower grade; the others had been commoners, and were thus absolute additions to the peerage. A Liberal marquis was made a duke solely because of his immense wealth, and the appointment was universally applauded, while a Conservative commoner found himself suddenly noble in all his veins because he had been Beaconsfield's private secretary.

In some few instances great military or naval

achievements have been rewarded with a peerage. Marlborough, Wellington, and Nelson are the famous names that will occur to all, and Strathnairn, Napier, and others in our own day have also fairly earned their rank by success in arms; but these can be counted on the fingers. The real passport to the upper House is the favor of the Prime Minister. Of course this may be won by public services; a great diplomatist or a successful Governor-General is sometimes ennobled, or raised a step in the peerage, but rarely unless he is of the party in power. There are besides what are called "law lords," lawyers who have risen from the middle, or even the lower, class by their ability or learning, and finally reached a seat in the House of Lords; but these must espouse a party, and have little chance of promotion while their antagonists are in possession of the Government. The bishops, too, and even the archbishops, are appointed by the Prime Minister from his own party in politics. The Father in God must be a Tory to be consecrated in Tory times, and a Liberal can succeed the Apostles only when the Liberals hold the reins. Nine-tenths of all the creations of peers in the last hundred years have been as purely for partisan reasons as the nominations of any President of the United States to which the advocates of "civil service reform" have been most violently opposed.

And these English appointments are not for a

term, nor for good behavior, but for life, and very often during very bad behavior; not only to executive, but to legislative office; not to one man, but to his descendants as long as the institutions of England endure. "When Pitt had been eight years in power," says an English writer, "he had created between sixty and seventy peers, of whom the greatest part owed their elevation to the Parliamentary support which they had themselves given to the Minister, or to their interest in returning members to the House of Commons. Can we wonder," he adds, "if some of them were unworthy of nobility?" This, however, was better than the action of the sovereigns themselves, when they were in reality, as well as in name, "the fountain of honor." Charles and James II. and George I. and II. all ennobled their mistresses. Most of the Kings have done the same for their illegitimate offspring, while many of the peerages conferred by James I. and Charles II. were sold.

On the other hand, no artist, no man of science, and, except Tennyson, no man of purely literary eminence, has ever received a coronet in England. Macaulay has sometimes been cited as an instance to the contrary; but had not his great genius been applied to politics, he never would have penetrated the House of Lords. It was the Whig partisan, not the brilliant essayist, not even the partial historian, who was rewarded with a peerage; and he would

not have received the dignity had he not b
childless and unmarried. For it is not unusual to
bestow this prize on an old and unmarried plebeian,
when it is probable that the title will become extinct upon his death. Thus the aristocracy is kept
exclusive, and if a man of the people finds his way
within the sacred purlieus, it is so contrived that he
shall not transmit his honors to another generation.

The distinctions among the aristocracy are numerous and intricate. The eldest son of a nobleman
of the rank of earl is "commonly called" by his
father's second title, for many peers are of several
degrees; the families have generally been ennobled
in a lower grade, and afterward risen to the rank
they now enjoy. Some of the dukes have thus half
a score of inferior titles, the Duke of Athole no
fewer than seventeen. The younger sons of dukes
and marquises use the prefix of Lord before their
Christian name, while the younger sons of earls and
all the sons of viscounts and barons have that of
Honorable. In nearly the same way the daughters
of dukes, marquises, and earls are called Ladies,
and the daughters of viscounts and barons Honorable. In all there must be eight or ten thousand
of these people, including the widows and children of deceased peers, who retain a diluted nobility. The grandchildren of peers are untitled,
but the eldest son of an eldest son, being in the
direct line of succession, has a place in the oligarchy.

Sometimes a man whose father is dead comes into a title transmitted from a more distant relative, an uncle or a cousin, and then, though he becomes a peer, his mother has not the rank which she would have enjoyed had he inherited from his father. Plain Mrs. Jones may have a son an earl, or even a duke. In such cases the brothers and sisters are raised to the rank of a peer's children; and the world calls them "paper" lords and ladies; but the mother does not receive the promotion, for she would then become a peeress without having married a peer.

Rank, however, descends below the nobility. The grade next to that of baron is baronet. This dignity is hereditary, but confers no right to a seat in the House of Lords. Its possessor bears the title of Sir before his Christian name, and his wife is called Lady. The first baronets were created by James I., and the title in his reign was often sold. At a time when the sovereign or the minister was lavish of the honor, a certain Duchess of Queensberry exclaimed that she could not spit out of her carriage window without spitting on a baronet. The famous Lady Holland of Holland House was almost as arrogant in our own day. She was a baroness, and Sir Henry Holland, the well-known physician and baronet, had been one of her favorite guests; but when she heard that he was about to marry, she declared that if he introduced another Lady

Holland into London society he should never enter her doors again. The dignity, however, is not a little prized by its possessors, of whom there were when I last counted no fewer than 873.

The lowest title of all is that of knight, which is not hereditary, and carries little distinction, but the knight is called Sir, and his wife Lady.

In society, titles are dropped as much as possible. Nobody nowadays says "your grace" to a duke or an archbishop, and to use "my lord" or "my lady," or "your lordship" or "ladyship" savors of the shop or the servants' hall. Neither do people of condition often talk of the Marquis of Bute or the Countess of Cork. Among themselves they say Lord Bute and Lady Cork. Indeed lord and lady are the appellations given in conversation to everybody in the peerage below the ducal rank. To a duke you say Duke, and to a duchess Duchess, though people not used to this high company often slip in a "grace" or two, to the amusement of their neighbors, but never that I could observe to the disturbance or surprise of the ducal personages themselves. These probably think the present familiarity with which people of their importance are addressed decidedly inappropriate. A certain duchess went not long ago to call upon a countess named Lady Cowper, but found she was mistaken in the person; and, expressing her regret, she said: "I suppose it was some inferior Lady Cowper I should have asked for." The peeresses, indeed, are not at all pleased that the wives of knights and baronets should take the title of Lady. The ancient form prescribed for these gentlewomen of lower degree was Dame, and the superior ladies think that their inferior sisters should retain the older appellation, so that the distinction in rank might be apparent. As it is, a marchioness may be confounded with the wife of an alderman, for either may be Lady Bath.

But the baronets' wives and the knights' wives like the custom very well. Most women prize rank more than men, and I once heard a close observer say that no woman in England would refuse a duke. I don't think he was right. Nevertheless, a woman who had earls for grandfathers on both sides of the house, but enjoyed no title herself, confessed to me that she was dying to be "My lady." I said to this scion of illustrious houses: "You surely wouldn't be the wife of a knight?" "Oh, yes, I would," she replied; "anything to be 'My lady.'"

Besides all these, there are various official people with temporary titles or precedence, but as a rule the members of the Government gain little in rank by being in office. The Prime Minister himself has no precedence by virtue of his place, and I have seen Mr. Gladstone, when at the head of the Government, go in to dinner after barons of his own creation. Even when ministers enjoy a temporary rank this never confers precedence on their wives, who, like the wives of bishops and archbishops, can sit at the bottom of the table and look up to the top, where their husbands are dining by the side of duchesses. When I first observed the little regard paid to official rank in England, I expressed my surprise, but was quickly told: "Oh! we respect the substance, not the shadow." An American would have said that rank was the shadow and power the substance, but hereditary, permanent rank is what most Englishmen prize above all earthly honors. It is the permanency, especially, that they value. The supercilious chamberlains of the English court would scoff at the punctilio of the officials in Washington, arranging themselves according to the grades of their short-lived grandeur.

Rank, indeed, in England is so much regarded that if the widow of a peer is remarried to a man of lower degree, she retains her former title in the later marriage. The famous Lady Waldegrave was married four times. By the second marriage she became a countess, and though afterward twice married to commoners, she remained a countess to the end. Her invitations at one time read: "Mr. Fortescue and Lady Waldegrave request the honor." Finally Mr. Fortescue was created Baron Carlingford, but still she retained her earlier title, for otherwise she must have descended to the rank of baroness. And this was in strict accordance with rule. The books lay down that as the nobility are all *pares*, peers, a peeress need not lose her higher rank because she is married to a nobleman of lower degree.

But this is law for the peers; it is not law for the commoners. Any woman, except a peeress who marries a peer, merges the highest rank she may have enjoyed in the dignity of her husband. The daughter of a marquis or a duke takes rank of a baroness, but if she marries a baron she forfeits her superior degree. There was an instance of this a few years ago, when the daughter of the Marquis of Ely married a Mr. Egerton. As her husband was a commoner, she preserved her precedence. They were Mr. and Lady Charlotte Egerton. But by and by Mr. Egerton was made a baron, and then Lady Charlotte applied to the Queen for permission to retain her former rank, but was refused. She was compelled to become a baroness.

A still more striking example of this extreme regard for precedence was that of Lady Stratheden, not now living. She was made a baroness in her own right, and subsequently her husband was created Baron Campbell. But Stratheden, being the older peerage by two or three years, had precedence of Campbell. So they went about as Lord Campbell and Lady Stratheden. But once, it is said, at an hotel, where the names were thus inscribed, the manager went to the husband and asked him quietly: "Couldn't you *call* her Lady Campbell?"

The same sentiment inspired the present Lord Chief Justice of England, who, when he was offered a peerage, requested that it should be given to his father; not from filial regard or reverence, but that he might himself inherit the title, and thus be the second lord. They dislike to be considered "creations." As the famous Lady Ashburton declared: "We don't like the honors that are earned." A still more important personage is said not long ago to have exclaimed: "The Garter is almost the only distinction left that those fellows of talent cannot gain." It is usually conferred on persons of at least the rank of duke, and rarely with any reference to ability or character. It is one of the honors that are not "earned."

## IV.

### PRIMOGENITURE.

THE aristocracy in England not only monopolizes the highest social honors of the kingdom, it possesses one-fifth of the soil, and is master of the time and services of immense numbers of the population, millions of whom live upon its estates or occupy its tenements, from the hovels of Killarney to the mansions of Belgravia. Although of late years the nobility has declined in political power, it still retains an important influence. One House of Parliament is composed exclusively of its members, and more than half the highest offices of every Government are taken from its body. It fills a large proportion of the best places in the Church, the army and the navy, and in diplomacy. It constitutes, with those whom it draws about it, and, directly or indirectly, influences and controls, what are called, and correctly, the governing classes of England.

The outward splendor of the peers may be imagined from the advice of the Shah of Persia to the Prince of Wales. That Eastern potentate had been entertained by the Duke of Sutherland at one of his estates, where the grounds and mansions were probably more palatial than any the royal savage had ever seen; and he is said to have declared to the Heir Apparent: " I should behead that duke. He is too magnificent for a subject." Something of the same sort, though probably not carried so far, must have been in Her Majesty's mind some years ago; for, as she was quitting a ball at Stafford House, another residence of the same nobleman, the sovereign said to the duchess: " I shall leave your palace and go home to my house."

In order to retain its importance, the aristocracy must be kept small in numbers, and this is accomplished by the infliction of immense wrongs upon the greater portion of its own members. Only one child can inherit the principal honors and possessions of the family. All the others are of inferior rank and consequence from their birth. In the enforcement of this rule the English aristocracy is more rigorous than any other in the world. The continental titles descend for the most part to all the children, and whole families continue noble for centuries. But the English maintain the importance of a house by the sacrifice of all its sons and daughters to the head. Even the wife of one peer and the mother of another is immolated on the altar of family pride. A woman who has been a duchess abdicates when her son comes to his title, she hands over the family jewels to her successor, is turned out of the mansion where she once presided, and although she retains the title of duchess, it is with the prefix of dowager, to indicate her fallen state; while the brothers and sisters, bred in luxury and splendor in their father's house, descend in one day to comparative indigence and insignificance. The brother thinks nothing of requiring them to leave, and they accept their fate as inevitable. They have always known it was to come, and are, perhaps, somewhat prepared for their downfall.

A nobleman now living is very generally censured because, having no sons, he has settled his unentailed estates upon his daughters, who thus will inherit fortunes which otherwise would have gone to his successor in the peerage. It is considered that he had no right to divert the estates away from the title, both having descended to him from the same ancestor. Even he, however, settled the bulk of his property on one daughter, leaving the other comparatively poor.

Circumstances and conditions like these necessarily have an unhappy effect upon the family relation. There cannot but be heart-burnings and discontent at the unnatural inequalities of fortune in a single household. The disparity between the deference paid to one brother by guests and servants, equals and dependants, and the indifference shown to another cannot but be galling to him who is set aside. The eldest son, even in childhood, knows that all is for him, that he is the superior. The younger children are early taught that they are only sojourners in their father's house, while their brother is a noble by birth, the future master and the head of the family. The next heir can hardly mourn very deeply if his elder brother dies, and there must be times when terrible temptations arise. A duke once said to a friend of mine, as his only son, a child of three years old, was taken out of the room: "There goes my natural enemy."

I remember the son of an earl talking to me with tears in his eyes of the lot of the younger members of a great family. He said he was repelled by the mothers whom he met in society as if he had the plague, lest he should fall in love with their daughters. He was to take his place almost without the sphere in which he had been born. He supposed he should become a steward on some nobleman's estate, or perhaps manage for his brother the property to which he was as much attached as the one who was to inherit all. But he suddenly checked himself, and declared that not for the world would he have it otherwise; nothing would compensate for the ruin of the old English families. The youngster was handsome, well-mannered, and evidently in love with some girl beyond his reach. He was cleverer by far than the man who would become the chief of his house, better fitted to bear the honors, but the accident of birth had intervened. It did not seem to him so great good fortune to be the son of an earl—so near the prize, and yet excluded from the race.

Nevertheless, the cadets of great houses are better off than if the aristocracy did not exist; better off than if they were humbler born. The sons and brothers of peers enjoy enormous advantages at the start. They have a high place in society, powerful friends, prestige, and sometimes opportunities to marry well, in spite of the dowagers. As a rule they are placed in the army or the Church, or pushed in politics or diplomacy, or possibly the law. Of late years, it is true, they have begun to take to trade, and there are sons of dukes who are " in tea." But this is not approved of in society, and aristocrats are not often reduced to such extremity.

After all, it is the mothers and daughters whose fate is most deplorable. Nothing in the whole system is so barbaric as the treatment of the women. Nothing is more pitiable than the lot of ladies delicately reared, accustomed from childhood to profusion and magnificence, and suddenly reduced to a pittance for an income. The daughters of a ducal house, the annual revenues of which cannot be less than a million of dollars, receive at their marriage, portions that do not amount to $3,000 a year; and this is considered a generous provision. I know a lady of less degree whose allowance from her father's estate is £200 a year, while her brother's is £10,000. For these unfortunates there is only one escape from comparative and often absolute poverty, and that is marriage. This is what makes the marriage market of London such a by-word. A well-known peeress, famous for the matrimonial successes of her daughters, is called in aristocratic circles "professional." The men declare it unfair in her to compete with amateurs, and I heard one of her acquaintances say that he was present the night she "caught York."

These high-born women must find husbands, or become enforced, and often unwelcome, pensioners on the bounty of brothers or more distant relatives. Then there is the mother, the great lady, superseded sometimes, not by the wife of her son, which would be more tolerable, but by some far-off cousin or life-long enemy. The dower-house is prepared, the dowry is paid, and she goes to her social suttee.

And it will not do to suppose that the head of a great family is always ready to assemble his relations about him, always willing to invite their visits or offer them homes. When a man comes into his titles and possessions he usually has his own wife and his own children to care for. The wife is indifferent to his kindred, and the new peer often forgets or ignores them altogether. The brothers and sisters and cousins of the master are hardly the most frequent visitors in great English houses; inmates they are more rarely still. And when they are received they are careful not to presume too far. They all look meekly up to their chief; they are proud to be connected with him, happy to accept his invitations and his charities. They are retainers and dependents, and there is and can be no equality between them, as a rule.

Of course, there are many families united by the warmest and purest regard. There are parents who insure their lives and economize their incomes in order to secure the independence of their younger children. There are great houses in which the chief considers himself bound to provide for and assist the cadets. The present Duke of Bedford, when he came into millions, settled on each of his brothers fifty thousand pounds. But conduct such as this is not the rule, and if it were, the influence of the institution remains, whatever the merit of the individual.

That influence makes the father lavish pride and affection and interest on the favored one, while even the mother, anticipating, perhaps, the time when he will be the arbiter of her fate, is careful not to thwart him in favor of her younger children. That influence makes the heir not seldom selfish, self-sufficient, over-bearing, and all the others subservient, or envious and dissatisfied. It makes marriages for money, among both men and women, common, and not altogether inexcusable. It made one duke regard his eldest son as his "natural enemy."

Primogeniture, however, in England, is matter of law. It cannot be avoided. If a man is born a peer, he must remain a peer, whether he likes it or no. He cannot be divested of the dignity, even though he may not choose to claim the title. In 1796 the Earl of Berkeley married a dairymaid, a previous marriage with whom was declared by the House of Lords "not proven," so that the children, born prior to 1796, could not inherit. The son first born after that date was of course the heir; but he refused to assume a title that reflected on his mother's fame—an act of chivalry seldom surpassed in the annals of any nobility. He died not long ago, having been known for more than half a century as the "Honorable Mr. Berkeley," though legally he was the sixth earl. But the title and honors descended to his heirs. He could not divert the succession. Nobility is in the blood, and nothing but an attainder can corrupt the quality.

Thus, distant descendants may claim a long-forgotten birthright, and titles and honors supposed extinct for centuries may be revived. The earldom of Devon had remained dormant from 1566 until 1831, when the heir, who was a clerk of the Parliament, and engaged in examining the records, discovered the original patent of the peerage. In ordinary cases the title descends to the heirs male "of the body" of the original patentee; but in this instance the words "of the body" did not occur. The title, therefore, descended to the heirs collateral, when those of the body became extinct. The last earl had died without issue in the reign of Bloody Mary (or, as the English more reverently style her, Mary I.), and the title and honors were supposed to be extinct. But when the patent was found the clerk of the Parliament was able to prove his descent in the collateral line, and was declared the lawful Earl of Devon after two hundred and sixty years. Meanwhile, the head of the family had been created a baronet, but, disdaining the inferior title, he never took out his patent. Nevertheless, he was always styled Sir William in commissions from the King, and his son was the second baronet. The antiquity of the family indeed reached back beyond the earldom. Edward I. was a legitimate ancestor, and Gibbon turns aside to record their history while reciting the fate of the Roman empire.

But though titles must descend according to the rule of primogeniture, the land can be entailed for three lives only. If a man dies without a will, his real estate falls to his eldest son, but a number of sudden deaths might prevent the heirs of important families from succeeding to the property. But titles without wealth would be barren honors; and to secure the all-important connection of property with rank a device has been contrived to which the aristocracy habitually resort, in evasion of the intention of the law. When the eldest son of a peer or important commoner marries, the custom is for the father and the son to unite in making an entail for their own lives and the life of the unborn son of the living heir. Thus every ordinary successor is born a tenant for life; he cannot himself alienate the property, and when he arrives at his majority he is ready in his turn to unite with his father to maintain the family dignity and provide for the greatness of one unborn child at the expense of all the others.

It is this principle of primogeniture, thus secured, which is at the basis of all the importance of the English aristocracy. Without it the nobility would promptly lose its pre-eminence. If all the descendants of a nobleman continued noble, the number would soon be so great that nobility would be no distinction. If all the children shared the wealth, the properties would be divided and subdivided till the pomp and circumstance of the peerage would disappear. It is because one man inherits all that the grandeur is permanent; because the heir has a quarter of a million a year, and his brother less than a thousand pounds, that the family dignity is maintained. When primogeniture is abolished the aristocracy will be near its fall.

## V.

### PRECEDENCE.

PRIMOGENITURE is the foundation on which the aristocracy is established, and the prop by which it is sustained; but precedence is the capital and crown of the edifice, the outward and visible sign by which as much as by pomp and show, the nobility asserts its superiority. For whoever acquires wealth, by whatever means, can of course command houses, estates, and retinues, and all the varied paraphernalia of luxury and display; but in England all this, without precedence, profiteth nothing. All the rest, to the ambitious aspirant, is but sounding brass and tinkling cymbals.

Precedence is not a matter of courtesy, nor often of mere custom, however ancient; it is the subject of absolute law. Its violation is actionable. One person is by law entitled to go before another person. The precedence of every individual of rank in the kingdom is regulated either by express statute, by letters patent, or by the common law. You will find it all set down in Blackstone and his successors. An earl of England goes before an earl of Scotland. A viscount's eldest son precedes an earl's younger sons. The daughters of a nobleman outrank the wives of the younger sons of the same peer. The intricacy is involved in the last degree, and when a woman of quality gives a dinner she often consults the books to settle the places of her company. For the married daughters of an earl must not be put before the unmarried daughters of a duke, nor the daughter of a peer of later creation before the daughter of one of the same rank whose creation is earlier. These are the ladies, a little distant from the sun, who insist most rigorously upon their reflected glories. Precedence, poor things, is all they have at times, and you cannot expect them to yield it readily.

There is, however, one result of the rage for rank that is refreshing. The precedence of the younger sons and daughters of the nobility continues through life. It matters not how poor they may become, their place and their titles remain; so that mere wealth cannot elbow aside the distinction that comes from lineage. No rich upstart can precede the broken-down woman of birth, and the fact that poverty and privation may coexist with even exalted rank depreciates the undue influence of mammon. The poor aristocrats can never lose their consequence in a society where a title may come to them suddenly by the death of a distant relative; and the mother of a possible duke must always be important to families whose daughters he may one day deign to ennoble.

For these potentates of the peerage can marry whom they please, and their wives step into the grade beside themselves. The Marquis of Salisbury is descended from the famous Lord Burleigh, so that his family has been noble since the time of Elizabeth, but he married the daughter of a lawyer. The wife afterward became intimate with a peeress more highly descended even than the late Premier. I asked this lady once whether her friend was of family that entitled her, according to English notions, to so grand an alliance; and she, herself sprung from royal lines, replied: "I mean to say that Lord Salisbury could marry whom he chose." As Marchioness of Salisbury the lawyer's daughter took precedence of her high-born friend.

She once had a greater triumph still. Many years ago her husband quarrelled with Lord Beaconsfield, but in 1874, when the Tories returned to power, it was found impossible for Beaconsfield to form a cabinet unless the two were reconciled. Great efforts were therefore made to bring them together. But Lord Salisbury was stubborn, and the same peeress assured me that the Duchess of Marlborough literally went on her knees to Lady Salisbury and implored her to persuade her husband to serve under his enemy. Lady Salisbury was won, Lord Salisbury consented, and, as a result, he became Prime Minister of England; for had he not submitted to Beaconsfield, he never would have succeeded him.

Precedence is a subject of so much consequence that no tribunal below the crown can be trusted to determine its finer points, and the difficult questions are referred in the last resort to the Queen, whose fiat in these matters is irreversible. Her Majesty fully realizes the importance of the prerogative, one of the few she yet retains in all its ancient plenitude, and devotes her best abilities to the distribution of justice in so grave a cause. But even into royal minds partiality will sometimes penetrate, and when her own family is concerned, the decisions of the sovereign have not always been received without suspicion of favor. She gave great offence by insisting that the Prince Consort should go before the Prince of Wales; and, had her husband lived, it is doubtful whether the English would have submitted to the regulation. The future king should have preceded his father, by all the unnatural rules of rank and royalty. More recently still Her Majesty has outraged the feelings, not only of her own nobility, but of the reigning families of Europe, by conferring the title of Royal Highness on the husband of her daughter Beatrice, when he has a right only to be called "Serene."

Precedence is a question that comes up constantly in all the ceremonies of the aristocracy; once a day, at least, to everybody, for everybody must dine, and everybody goes to dinner according to degree. I have seen at German watering-places English women of birth, sisters and sisters-in-law, as punctilious in yielding and taking place at a *table d'hôte* as if they had been at court. The last night I dined in England two earls were leaving the room together, and as the one whose rank was more recent held back for his senior, he said laughingly, but he meant it all the same: "I must not go before my betters."

Americans, even, may become involved in the labyrinthine mysteries. An American envoy was once visiting at a famous house where the Lord Lieutenant of the county was also a guest, and the hostess went to dinner, according to rule, with the minister. But at this the wife of the Lord Lieutenant was up in arms; she searched the books and declared that her husband represented the Queen, and therefore should precede a foreign minister. The gentlemen staying at the house also looked up the authorities, but disagreed with her. Still she remained dissatisfied, until finally the hostess went to the minister and begged him, in order to pacify the punctilious peeress, to allow the Lord Lieutenant to precede him for a single night; and the American was amiable, and waived his privilege. I think I said that precedence is not controlled by courtesy.

Another time it was the minister's wife who insisted on her prerogative. For Americans who live in this atmosphere are susceptible to the influence. One of our representatives was staying at a ducal house, and the first night the duke took in the minister's wife to dinner; but the next night, to vary or divide his courtesies, he offered his arm to another lady, whereat the minister's wife was wroth, and, being the head of her own family, she insisted on leaving the house, and the democratic envoy cut short his visit because his wife was not taken in every night at the head of the company.

These difficulties extend into the loftiest regions. The Viceroy of Ireland represents Her Majesty, and during his term has precedence even of the Prince of Wales. It is said that the Heir Apparent dislikes to visit Ireland because he is unwilling to follow the Viceroy. This functionary, indeed, has a little court of his own, where, as in all provincial circles, the etiquette is stiffer than in grander spheres. When the Viceroy dines out everybody rises as he enters the room, and when the ladies leave the table each approaches and makes him in turn the courtesy that is due to royalty. Even his wife must do this in public, though I doubt if she does it at home.

I have known earls take their own daughters to table, because these were of higher rank than any one else in the room; and at royal houses the hosts invariably precede their guests, unless the guests themselves are royal. I have even seen a child go in to dinner at the head of a distinguished company. At a country-house where a foreign minister and his wife were guests, the host had not returned from the hunting-field in time for dinner. There were several members of the Government present, men of title and consideration in English circles; but the ladies of the family sent to the school-room for the eldest son, a boy of thirteen, to represent his father, and he, as a viscount, took precedence of all the gentlemen present, and offered his arm to the wife of the minister.

As a rule, scant deference is shown to Americans in this matter of precedence. Neither hospitality nor courtesy is said to be in question, but the law. Now, the law may be very well for Englishmen, by whom and for whom it was made, but it can hardly apply to foreigners who are neither referred to in its provisions nor comprehended in its denominations or degrees. The English, however, habitually apply their own rules and their own ideas on every subject to everybody else. They recognize neither military, nor literary, nor even political distinction among themselves when there is question of rank; a general goes behind his own aid-de-camp if the latter is a lord and the general is not; the greatest writer in the land, Browning or Froude, or, until the other day, Tennyson, would be preceded by any blockhead of a baron; and the Prime Minister, if a commoner, gives way to peers of his own creation. So, American gentlemen, and ladies too, of whatever consideration at home, are usually sent to the foot of the table, because they possess no English titles. European dignities are recognized, for they correspond to those in the English peerage, but our unofficial countrymen do not usually fare so well. Both ex-President Fillmore and ex-President Pierce were in London soon after the expiration of their terms of office, and dined at different times with different Ministers for Foreign Affairs. Each was sent to table without a lady and behind the rest of the company. They were plain gentlemen, it was said, and, "if the Americans give their ex-Presidents no rank, why should we?" General Grant, it is true, except in one conspicuous instance, was given precedence of everybody in England below the royal family, but his case had neither parallel nor precedent.

There are, however, English houses where simply as strangers the place of honor is given to Americans. This is, of course, among people who have seen much of the world, and discovered that even in civilized nations usages may exist different from those of England, and that persons of consequence can be found in other countries who yet are not the bearers of English titles. The greater the house the greater the consideration an American is likely to receive. If he dines with a duke, the chances are that he will go in with the duchess; if the host is a recent arrival in the great world, he may have no lady, and will probably enter last.

But the rule does not always hold. I was dining once with a woman of rank who was also a personal friend. The company included two marquises, one of whom was a cousin of the hostess and a man of cosmopolitan breeding. Before dinner this nobleman came up to me and said:

"I have been telling my cousin that you ought to take her in, but she says 'No;' she likes you very well, but you can't go before a marquis. I insisted that, as a foreigner and an official, you should precede; but she will not yield."

Mr. Lecky, the historian, was present, and I was then new in English society; so, with all the simplicity of a republican, I replied:

"Mr. Lecky is the most distinguished man in the room. Shouldn't he take Lady Mary?"

But the liberal marquis at once exclaimed:

"Oh! Mr. Lecky is an Englishman. He must take his place."

So Lady Mary went in with a vapid youth of twenty-two, because he was a marquis, and the most eminent person at dinner had no lady, and went last.

## VI.

### THE PRINCE OF WALES.

I SHALL never forget the scene in St. Paul's Cathedral when the highest personages in England were gathered to attend the Thanksgiving for the recovery of the Prince of Wales from a serious illness. The immense building was crowded to its utmost capacity. Nave and choir and aisles, and even galleries erected for the occasion, were thronged with patricians and functionaries of importance; clergymen and prelates and lawyers and judges in their gowns; officers of the army and navy in full uniform; peers and the eldest sons of peers and members of the House of Commons in levee dress. Every one was in his place by nine o'clock, and the doors were closed hours before the Queen arrived. The great space under the dome was allotted to members of Parliament and the diplomatic corps, and in the centre of this area a dais had been erected, covered with crimson cloth and ruled off with gilded bars to form a sort of pew. The floor of this structure was so high that its occupants stood with their feet on a level with the heads of the peers and the members of the Government, and into the pew thus raised the Queen and the royal family were ushered, every one in the edifice rising. The son of an earl shook up the cushions, and the Archbishop of Canterbury thanked God in the name of the people of England for the recovery of the young man of twenty-eight or twenty-nine, who, with his mother and brother and sisters, knelt above the heads of the nobility and the Government.

But this enforced prostration of all the distinction and dignity of England at the very feet of the royal family in the house of God was the merest of mockeries. The Queen herself is only the shadow of a potentate, and the Prince of Wales is insignificant in everything but ceremony. An absolute abstinence from politics is dictated by the nation, not only to the sovereign, but to the entire reigning family. It is not thought proper for the Prince of Wales to signify a preference for either party in the State. He holds his place on condition that he makes no effort to influence affairs; he must be as gracious to a Conservative minister as to a Liberal; he must take sides neither for nor against any prominent measure. The pill is gilded by the assurance that he belongs to the whole country, and not to a part; that he is above the strife of factions, and too great to be interested in intrigues for place. All of which may be true, but it leaves him a vapid and meaningless life, devoted to forms and filled up with frivolities.

The Queen, indeed, goes through the ceremonies of authority; she holds privy councils and receives ambassadors; and, if not present at cabinet meetings, the result of them is usually announced to her before it is made known to the world at large. She reads despatches, and still, at times, discusses measures of importance with the Prime Minister. But the Prince of Wales, the future King, is never summoned to her counsels. She seems to revenge herself on him for the exclusion from power inflicted on herself. There is no pretence of consulting him. He can hardly be familiar with the forms in which he must one day bear a part, or, so far as practice goes, with the principles by which he must be guided. He will come to the throne as utterly unaccustomed to its graver duties as his own son, if at any moment both Queen and Prince of Wales were suddenly to die. Opportunities for observation, of course, he shares with everybody in the kingdom; good sense he has not often seemed to lack; appreciation of the difficulties and delicacies of his political situation he has repeatedly displayed to a greater degree than the Queen; but the absolute experience which he might have acquired had he, the immediate heir to the throne, a man of more than forty years, been summoned to the royal side in interviews with ministers, or consultations such as must occur under even a constitutional monarchy between sovereign and statesmen—of this he has been altogether deprived.

Whether it is the ordinary jealousy of a monarch for an heir, which has prevailed against the wisdom of a ruler and the partiality of a parent, or some other cause, I never heard; but the fact remains, that the Prince of Wales has had no opportunity to learn from his mother the lessons in practical sovereignty which the Queen herself received from her sagacious consort, or has acquired from the experience of nearly half a century.

This is unfortunate for the Prince himself, for the country, and for the ministers who may hereafter have to deal with him. I once asked a prominent Englishman what would happen if a prince should come to the throne, ambitious at once and able, determined to rule as well as to reign. My friend at first answered evasively that there was no danger of the conjuncture under the present family; but when I pressed him further, he admitted that, in such an event, the monarch, if he persisted, would lose his crown. Nobody tells a prince such things in ordinary conversation, but the warning might be conveyed if he were present when the Queen is sometimes delicately informed of the necessity of subordinating her will to that of the nation. The Heir Apparent is surrounded by servitors and courtiers, always bowing and backing out before him, till he might easily forget the emptiness of the forms and the impotence of the sway to which he will succeed; and if he were not alive to the reality, a harsh awakening might one day come to him.

It must, however, be acknowledged that His Royal Highness is scrupulous in conforming to the political necessities. He betrays no preferences, except personal ones, to which he has a right. He involves himself in no difficulties with either party in politics, he makes no attempt to step beyond the limits laid down for him, and confines himself strictly to the ceremonious and arduous life of pleasure and parade which his fate and his mother have decided that he shall lead. It is often said that he does not expect to succeed to the throne, but lives in dread of the evil day that has come to so many of his royal relatives. Apparently, he is determined to do nothing himself to precipitate the political deluge.

Debarred from all participation in affairs of state, he has become a great authority in etiquette. Both the Queen and the Prince of Wales devote themselves to the study of this great science with a fervor that makes it the important business of their lives. Perhaps it compensates for the sacrifice of higher ambitions; and in settling points of precedence and determining questions of ceremony they may seem to themselves to retain some of the prerogatives of Henry VIII. and Elizabeth. The

Queen corrects the court circular daily; she arranges the order in which the guests sit at her table; she supervises the invitation lists to court balls—at which she never is present—and the Prince carefully inspects the book kept at his gate, in which visitors inscribe their names.

Sometimes the royal personages do not agree on points of this high consequence, and then Her Majesty asserts the supremacy of the Crown. You cannot be asked to the Queen's ball unless you have been at court the same year. For very great personages the rule may be relaxed, but in ordinary cases it is immutable. Once upon a time, however, a fair American arrived too late in the season for a drawing-room, and, in spite of etiquette, she determined to go to a ball. But the American Minister declined to ask the court to break its own regulations, and our undaunted countrywoman, who had met the Heir Apparent in society, applied to the Prince himself. His Royal Highness likes pretty women, and pretty Americans quite as well as any others; so he good-naturedly promised that if the American Minister would make the request the invitation should arrive. But when this was announced to the wily diplomatist from the United States, that functionary still had the fear of the court before his eyes, and with the art of a Machiavelli he wrote to the Lord Chamberlain that, " at the instance of the Prince of Wales he had the honor to apply, etc."

The card was sent and the importunate American went to the ball. But the august Queen of Great Britain and Ireland was indignant at the infringement on her prerogative. She informed the heir to the throne that the ball was her ball, not his; and the Prince was vexed with the minister, and the minister was vexed with his compatriot; and altogether the excitement aroused in exalted circles was very like what occurred at Olympus when Juno and her progeny were interested in the affairs of earth and the gods took different sides.

The lot of the Prince is not without other trials. Nobody in the kingdom is harder worked or undergoes more fatigue of a certain wearing sort than the Prince and Princess of Wales, and in a less degree the other members of the reigning family. They are not only deprived of all privacy, not only always in the world and before the world, always attended by persons of consequence and exposed to comment and criticism from fastidious tastes and censorious tongues, but they are dragged from one ceremony to another, from a gallery to a hospital, from a levee to a procession, from a dinner to a ball, till life must often become a weariness. Yet they must never fail to keep an engagement, and they are bound always to display the especial "politeness of kings"—punctuality. They must be civil when they are worn out, and gracious when they are sleepy; they must remember the names and faces of the tens of thousands to whom their recognition is an honor; for all this is their trade. This is how they earn their living. And they play their part well. They are trained to it from childhood. They do remember people; they are punctual and polite; all of which should be borne in mind when people carp and criticise.

The Prince is personally popular among those who surround him closest. His invitations are an honor as well as a command, and when he visits a country-house the list of the guests who are to meet him is submitted for his inspection. The Princess does not always accompany her consort on these occasions. As sometimes happens with families that are not royal, there are houses favored by the husband which the wife does not frequent, though not so many of these as when the Prince was younger. They both seem to have their American favorites. A number of our compatriots have been asked, not only to Marlborough House, but to Sandringham; but it must be owned these have sometimes been ladies and gentlemen at whose success Americans at home were not a little surprised. The Prince, however, cares nothing for the social antecedents of his transatlantic friends. He cannot distinguish the delicate gradations in a democratic society so visible to some of the democrats themselves. When he was told by a Bostonian whose family had been "good" for nearly three generations that the American

Minister of that day was a self-made man, the Prince replied to the aristocratic republican: "I thought you were all self-made in America."

Perhaps the Prince is not to be blamed. He lives in an atmosphere where incense is constantly offered him, and dukes and duchesses prostrate themselves before the royal family with something of the idea of Bunthorne in "Patience": "If this great personage is too great for me, what a very great personage this personage must be!"

For the reverence shown by the aristocracy for royalty is greater than that of the people at large. The people generally know very little about royalty. The Queen secludes herself, and the other members of the royal family live so far apart from and above the multitude that they hardly enter its thoughts. But the nobility have the Queen and her children constantly in mind. They must go to levees and drawing-rooms; they are invited to state balls and concerts. The personal attendants of royalty are taken exclusively from the aristocracy. During the London season the members of the aristocracy are continually meeting the royal family, and constantly reminded of the vast difference in rank between the highest of themselves and the Princes of the Blood.

The genuflections they must make in the presence of royalty; the deference in tone and manner they must display if addressed by royalty; the red carpet that must be laid down when royalty visits a house; the ceremonies of reception and departure; the separate table at which royalty must eat at great entertainments; the fact that one should not leave a room until royalty chooses to do so; that one cannot speak first, nor broach a subject of conversation with royal personages; that you must neither present yourself to them, nor by any chance turn your back toward them; even the apparently insignificant matter that you say "Sir" to a Prince, and "Madam" or "Ma'am" to the Queen and the Princesses, and to nobody else in England—all this deepens the impression on an ordinary mind, and makes many look up to the members of the royal family with an obsequiousness which, to one who does not share it, is amusing.

One of the most eminent of British statesmen once said to me: "Every Englishman is at heart a lackey. We all want something above us; something to—to——" He hesitated for a word, and I suggested: "To kotow to?"

"Yes," said he, "to kotow to."

## VII.

### AMERICANS AT COURT.

The whole happiness of the American Minister to England is marred by the ever-recurring necessity of presenting his country people at court. Most Americans abroad consider that the principal business of their representatives is to procure them invitations to balls or tickets to picture galleries. The London Legation is especially beset with genteel but importunate democrats, determined to explore the mysteries that surround the effete institutions of royalty, to behold in person the gold sticks-in-waiting, the gentlemen-at-arms in their helmets and plumes, the maids of honor, and the mistresses of the robes.

They might, it is true, do all this from a position in the palace galleries, out of which respectable English folk not grand enough themselves to go to court are content to look upon the procession of their betters as it passes toward the inner apartments. But no true American acknowledges any "betters;" the very word is stricken from our prayer-books. The citizens of the great republic will stand in no outer galleries; they must be ushered into the very presence-chamber of royalty.

No other minister is so subject to this demand. It is only once in a while that the ambassador from Russia or Germany is called upon to present a countryman to the Queen. Aristocrats, apparently, are not so anxious as republicans to frequent foreign courts. They are familiar with the spectacle and fatigued with the etiquette at home. Besides which, only those entitled to be presented to their own sovereign can be received by the English Queen, and the regulations at Berlin and St. Petersburg are as rigid as at St. James's, so that applications from Russians or Germans are rare. But every decent American may know the Chief Magistrate of the Union, and therefore, according to the rules, he is authorized to ask for a presentation to the Queen. Remembering the levees at Washington, one can imagine the perplexities of the envoy of a democracy.

But this is not all. The court regulations declare that ladies and gentlemen "of distinction" can be presented by their minister in the diplomatic circle, a privilege which entitles them to remain in the presence-chamber during the entire levee or drawing-room, and usually secures an invitation to a ball. Now as all Americans in Europe are persons of distinction, they naturally all desire to be presented with the diplomatic corps. The women especially, fashionable, or would-be fashionable, insist upon this recognition, and besiege the unlucky minister, whose torments can be more easily imagined than endured.

American women, however, invariably dress well; much better, as a rule, than the English ladies who go to court. They also adapt themselves with marked facility to unfamiliar circumstances; and as they have only to courtesy and pass before the Queen, there is little opportunity to do discredit to their country or its representative. It is from no fear of a blunder or a scene that the minister is concerned. It is the numbers from whom he must choose that are so appalling. For, after all, the drawing-room is for English subjects, and as there are always more of these than Her Majesty desires to see on such occasions, it is rather hard for her and for them to give up the precious time to foreigners.

In self-defence, therefore, and in accordance with the traditions of their craft, the wily American diplomatists have contrived to fence themselves about with rules. They have entered into a pact with the court functionaries, themselves nothing loath, by virtue of which only four men and four women can be presented at one time with the diplomatic corps, and the same number in what is called the "general circle." The roster of men is often incomplete, but the occasion is rare when the eight ladies are not all on hand. The minister usually requires a letter of introduction from a personal acquaintance before sending in the name of one entirely unknown to him. But I sometimes used to think that the lists were declared full very early in the season, although if any one whom the minister particularly wished to place came later, a place was found without all the difficulty that might have been anticipated.

But the gravest question of all is where to draw the line between those who are of sufficient "distinction" to be presented in the diplomatic circle and those who are relegated to "the general." Most ministers cut the matter short by announcing that, as we have no rank nor class distinctions in America, presentations in the diplomatic circle must be restricted to official persons and their families— governors of States, senators, high military or naval officers, and the like. Of course stray friends of the minister himself slip in occasionally, whose claim might be disputed, but to be a cousin of an envoy, or even of an acting chargé d'affaires, is to be a "person of distinction," at least in the eyes of him who is to decide. The court takes him for sponsor, and I never heard but once that a presentation requested by an American minister was refused.

The court, indeed, is very good to Americans. It does not inquire if they are engaged in trade, although no English merchant can be presented to his sovereign without especial claim. It looks not too closely to the morals or the manners of our countrymen or country-women, but very carefully to their clothes. The rules for dress are never relaxed for any Americans except those in the legation. All men must wear knee-breeches and swords, the court costume, or uniform. As for the women, they are only too happy to put on feathers and trains and any other frippery that etiquette will authorize.

But still another difficulty sometimes remains before an American lady with her unwilling guide arrives at the threshold of the court. A minister can present only men: and the Queen refuses to allow to the daughters of a diplomatist the precedence of a minister's wife or the privilege of presenting her compatriots, so that if the envoy is unmarried he must find some friendly matron to perform the office for him. For a long time it was customary, as it certainly was becoming, in such a crisis, to ask this favor of the wife of the English Minister for Foreign Affairs, and the request was gracefully and graciously complied with. A few years ago, however, a woman whose husband was Foreign Secretary declined to consider herself bound to present American ladies to the Queen, though vouched for by the American representative. There have been times when such a refusal would have produced a rupture in the relations of sovereign States; but the American Minister meekly submitted to the slight, and had recourse to other ladies of his acquaintance. He always found them willing. Sometimes it was the wife of a colleague in the diplomatic corps who came to his relief; sometimes an English woman who atoned for the discourtesy of her compatriot.

When every preliminary is settled the persistent fair one, triumphing over the last obstacle, proceeds to Buckingham Palace, not, however, with her minister or with the lady who is to present her, but in her own carriage, for the furbelows and feathers take up a deal of room, and two ladies dressed for court will crowd the largest coach. If she is to be presented in the diplomatic circle her servant has a ticket admitting her carriage at a special entrance; she then need not fall into line a mile from the palace, but drives direct to the Ambassadors' door, and waits only a few moments in the ante-room. Then she follows her sponsor, and remains with her to the end.

If she goes to the general circle she must take her place in St. James's Park, or still further away, prepared to wait patiently for hours, while the rabble stare in at her carriage windows and comment audibly upon her charms, her laces, and her jewelry, guessing at her age or the prices of her clothes.

Nor is it only the outside mob that indulges in these investigations. One of our country-women told me of an experience she had in the precincts of royalty that is worth recording. She had arrived at "the pens," as the ante-chambers are irreverently called by those who frequent them. Tired of standing for hours, jostled and trodden on and stared at by high-bred dames, the American was about to retire from the column, when a lively contest of voices immediately in her rear attracted her attention.

"I tell you it is."

"No, it cannot be."

"But look for yourself."

Turning to learn the cause of the dispute, the stranger found two English ladies turning up her train to discover whether or no it was lined with lace. Fortunately for her feminine pride the lace was real.

The ball, the object of all these efforts and importunities, is very much like other balls. The dresses of the men are more showy than at a private party in America; but those of the women not so brilliant, except that finer jewelry is worn. Court trains are not prescribed, nor are feathers indispensable, though the men are not admitted except in uniform or court-dress. I once saw an exception to this rule. The Emperor of Brazil wore a black coat and trousers and heavy boots at one of these balls. But His Imperial Majesty constantly violated not only etiquette, but good breeding as well. He was above the rules.*

Every one is supposed to be in the room before the entrance of royalty, and at about ten o'clock "God Save the Queen" is struck up, and the Princess of Wales with her ladies heads the procession. Afterward come the Prince of Wales, his brothers, and their attendants; for in all court ceremonies the women of equal rank precede the men. I was once at a dinner given to an Emperor and Empress,

---

* Before Dom Pedro's arrival in England, the Brazilian minister had issued cards for a ball in his master's honor, to which all the great people in London were asked; but when the Emperor came to town he declared that the minister had no right to make arrangements for him without his knowledge, and refused to go to the ball. So the servant was disgraced before the world, though he had shown himself a finer gentleman than the sovereign whom he had sought to please.

Another instance of the imperial discourtesy will be more interesting to Americans. General Grant arrived in London a week earlier than the Emperor. He had welcomed Dom Pedro to America the year before as President, and paid him every attention due from one Head of a State to another. He now sent to inquire when it would suit the Emperor to receive a visit. His Majesty was not in, and the message was delivered to a Chamberlain. But the Emperor never made any reply to the offered courtesy, and the visit was not paid.

where the Prince of Wales entered first, preceding even the Emperor, because he walked with the Empress.

After a few moments the first quadrille is formed, in which no one joins but royalty, or those whom royalty invites; afterward dancing becomes general, but the upper part of the room is appropriated to the court and persons of very high rank. If a princess wishes to dance with a nobleman or gentleman, she sends him word by an equerry, for no one not royal can ask her. So also, when a prince desires a partner of lower degree, his lord-in-waiting signifies the princely pleasure, though the royal brothers sometimes overlook this form and invite in person the lady with whom they deign to dance. Needless to say, they are never refused.

The ball-room is oblong in shape, and showily, rather than splendidly decorated, according to the taste of the Prince Consort, which was always heavy and gaudy in art. At the top of the room, and running nearly across it, is a dais, with chairs of state for the royal personages; and on each side of this, but at right angles, are several tiers of seats, those on one side reserved for the diplomatic corps, on the other for peeresses; the bench next the floor for duchesses, the next for marchionesses, and so on; and it is amusing to observe how scrupulous these noblewomen are to take exactly the place to which they consider themselves entitled. The court has never recognized the right of the duchesses to the seats they claim; but every duchess insists upon her bench, and royalty winks at the usurpation.

After the first quadrille it used to be the custom when I first went to court (it is different now) for the greatest personages to pass in line before the Princes, who, to receive this homage, ranged themselves standing along the dais. The diplomatic corps went first, the ladies leading the way; then the men of the corps, according to their rank and the seniority of their standing at the English court. Afterward the duchesses advanced. The dais was so high that as they made their courtesies the heads of the ladies were brought about to the knees of the Princes. Some of these peeresses were of lineage as ancient as that of the royal family, and descended from as many kings; others were the wives and daughters of men whose estates are larger than German principalities, and whose incomes transcend those of all the children of the Queen; while for public service and character, their names will live when the world has forgotten whether Victoria was ever married. But the prostration went on, and those who performed it seemed as satisfied as those who received.

At midnight supper is served, and, of course, royalty precedes. The doors of the supper-room are at the sides of the dais, and the great folk who usually surround royalty are already near these doors. And now comes one of the most extraordinary of all the scenes in court life. Only the most distinguished in rank are supposed to follow the Princes to the supper-room. The doors are very soon closed, and the struggle among duchesses and ambassadors and people of that sort to get within these portals in time is something more ridiculous and unrefined than is ordinarily supposed to occur in palaces. You can see nothing worse in any parvenu house in the Fifth avenue.

Once in, the aristocracy smooths its ruffled plumage, and places itself in two parallel lines, to watch the royal hosts at their repast, for no guest can be served till the Princes are appeased. There are three tables lining three sides of the room, and the royal family advance to the centre one, where they stand with their backs to the company, looking for all the world like ordinary people at an ordinary table at an ordinary ball. After the hosts have satisfied themselves they turn to their guests, and pass leisurely down the room toward the entrance, while the magnates of England in rank and political power and territorial importance press gently forward, if haply they may catch a royal glance and perform the profound genuflection again.

Sometimes a scion of royalty feels a desire to stop and exchange a word with an individual of sufficient consequence, and then the favored one bends deferentially forward, the object of envy all along the line. When the Prince or Princess thinks the colloquy has been sufficiently prolonged a little signal makes the participant aware that this high honor and happiness is over; another profound obeisance, and the man or woman whom royalty has recognized sinks back into the crowd, beaming with reflected radiance.

At other times the Princes walk steadily by, conversing with each other, and ignoring every highbred effort to attract their notice, and then the lines of courtiers on both sides all bow together very low, like the chorus in the opera bouffe of "Barbe Bleue," and pretend not to be disappointed; but when the children of the Queen have passed along their lieges fall to discussing their faults as vigorously as if the hosts were mortal, like themselves. In all these abasements I never noticed that the ultra-Radicals who go to court were any less supple than the most ardent Tories, while the last manufacturer who had entered the Government craned his neck for recognition as eagerly as the American Minister or the oldest groom of the stole.

## VIII.

### THE CROWN IN POLITICS.

If all the parade of obeisance that surrounds the Queen indicated the real power of a mighty sovereign, even democrats might appreciate the pageantry. If Victoria were an Elizabeth and could send her nobles to the Tower, if she possessed the authority of Kaiser or Czar, or one tithe of the influence in public affairs of an American President, the shows of supremacy would have significance. Prerogative may be arrogant without pretension, and autocracy is not ridiculous, however imperious. But the abject statesmen, who sat at the feet of their mistress at St. Paul's were Mayors of the Palace after all. It is the change of a ministry, not the death of a sovereign, that convulses England.

I was talking once with a Prime Minister, who declared that the great fault in American institutions is the quadrennial change of Presidents and the political turbulence that attends it. "Nothing like this," he said, "occurs when an English sovereign dies." I could not refrain from answering that the parallel did not hold. The real crisis in

England is when a government goes out of power, not when a monarch leaves the scene. The statesman was silent. He could not deny that his own downfall would be a greater event than the demise of his mistress and the transfer of the regalia to another wearer. These are but the trappings and the suits of power.

Lord Beaconsfield could make the Queen into an Empress, and the Government of the day settles the allowance of every royal prince when he arrives at his majority, as well as the dowry of every princess at her marriage. It even determines the income of the sovereign upon an accession to the throne. The Queen cannot create a peer against the will of the Prime Minister. If he makes out a list of his adherents to be elevated to the Upper House, Her Majesty is sometimes permitted to add the name of a personal friend, but not too often. She can refuse her sanction to no measure which the Government approves. Her speeches from the throne are all written for her. She must even accept distasteful ministers if the House of Commons or the nation will have no others.

The Queen, nevertheless, declines to consider herself a mere mouthpiece for her ministers. A few years ago I was staying at the house of a member of the government who had just returned from Balmoral—for a minister is always in attendance on the Queen to lay public business before her and procure her signature to public documents. My host assured me that Her Majesty took the liveliest interest in national affairs, that she studied closely all matters of importance, had opinions of her own and expressed them freely, and sometimes induced her ministers to change their minds. Her long experience and acquaintance with political men give her some advantages that none of her subjects can enjoy. She has never been out of office, and she knows the secrets of both the great parties in the State.

Until quite recently, however, the ordinary Englishman supposed his sovereign to be excluded from all participation in politics, a mere puppet, whose strings the minister pulled. But when the Memoirs of Baron Stockmar, the tutor of the Prince Consort, appeared, they divulged the fact familiar to the initiated, that both the Queen and the Prince had always entertained decided opinions on political subjects, and more than once had attempted to affect, and even to change, the foreign policy of England. Diplomacy, indeed, is the sphere in which the Queen especially aspires to exert an influence. Her foreign connections by blood and marriage undoubtedly contribute to mould her opinions: and she dislikes, besides, to appear to foreign sovereigns to possess less weight in the affairs of her own kingdom than they enjoy in theirs. So she keeps up a correspondence on state matters with kings and emperors which she fancies is of importance, and which may, indeed, sometimes have had its influence; though doubtless the Bismarcks and Gortchakoffs have been careful to discount the feminine diplomacy at its actual value.

The discovery of this royal intervention created not only widespread surprise, but unfavorable, and even hostile, comment among her subjects; for there are not a few in England, and their number increases every year, who hold the functions of a constitutional sovereign to consist in simply signing, with closed eyes and lips, whatever document a minister may present. They submit to monarchy only on condition that its claws shall be closely pared. But now the Queen stood revealed as something more than a figurehead; the machine was an automaton, but with a concealed workman; for her judgment, it was seen, had been not merely guided, but controlled, by her foreign husband, while the Prince himself had relied in a great measure on the advice of his German mentor, Baron Stockmar, an individual of whose very existence nine-tenths of the British nation had been unaware.

These disclosures were at first distasteful to the court, which, at least in the Prince Consort's time, had been content with a share of power without the show; but when once the real state of affairs was unveiled a bold face was put on the matter. In the "Life of the Prince Consort," written not only with the sanction, but with the avowed assistance of the Queen, the doctrine was defended that the sovereign of right should have opinions, and maintain them, too, on all subjects of national importance. One volume of this work appeared at the height of the controversy in regard to the Turco-Russian war; and the leaning of the court in that controversy was purposely and unmistakably made apparent.

The result was proof that no serious intervention of the Crown will ever be tolerated in English politics again. The interposition in this instance was very generally regarded as injudicious, and by many was resented as an unwarrantable encroachment; while the dislike which in various quarters had been felt for the character and policy of Lord Beaconsfield was in some degree extended to the Queen. At no time during my long residence in England was there so much of downright animosity displayed toward the court. Politicians wantonly fanned the flame for selfish or party purposes, and courtiers foolishly followed their example, dragging Majesty itself into the strife. Lord Beaconsfield, one of the ablest and most unscrupulous adventurers who ever rose to power, was directly answerable for this opposition toward the Queen. He deliberately used his influence with a weak old woman, beguiling her by flattery and a show of deference for her opinions, to assume an authority that he knew the nation would resent; an authority which he was himself to exercise, while the opinions were those that he had himself infused.

With a few in England—the courtiers and those who aspire to be courtiers—the sentiments of the sovereign still have weight. Here and there a genuine Tory survives who believes in the divine right of kings, because that implies the divine right of dukes and earls and landed gentry and superiors generally. The nobility, as a class, perceive that their cause is bound up with that of the throne; that if one is overturned, the other must roll in the dust; if one is maintained, the other is likelier to remain secure. Like the priests of a false religion, they fall down before the image they have themselves set up, and, in the eyes of the multitude, are its profoundest worshippers. It is with this feeling that they behave toward the Queen as if she were the Grand Lama of Thibet, and keep up the mummeries that have been discarded by the Mikado of Japan. Perhaps at times the homage is in part sincere. People often persuade themselves of what they wish to believe, and by dint of repeating a form one may come to accept a creed.

There are others who see through the sham, but go through the show all the same; the courtiers who are so close as to perceive the nakedness of royalty under its robes, or the aspirants and adventurers who are aware that this is the way to make themselves acceptable to their social superiors.

Lord Beaconsfield was chief among these, and knew how to use the others; to form a party out of them, and to crowd himself to the head of the party. He was so much cleverer than any one else in England, that he, the most un-English of English statesmen, of a hated race and hostile creed, without either the nobler qualities or the adventitious aids that Englishmen seem equally to reverence, without family or fortune, or political honesty or consistency, was able to make himself the leader of the aristocracy of England; to represent and to control both the Tories and the Crown. Knowing full well that the course to which he advised the Queen was sure to prove in the end injurious to the Crown, that to thrust Majesty at the people at this day was to endanger its existence, he yet believed that the danger would not come nor the storm burst in his time. He could and would retain power and place by pandering to the vanity of the Queen and playing on the loyalty of her subjects, and on the veneration of the English people for whatever is established.

For a while the scheme worked well. The influence of the Crown helped him to gain voters in Parliament, though he lost them out of it; and he had the sagacity, besides, to appeal to the imperial instinct in Englishmen as well as to the national pride, combining these in his own designs, and making them the tools to contribute to his supremacy. He carried his measures for a day.

The Queen had no longer the calm judgment and the strong good sense of the Prince Consort to lean upon, and, woman-like, allowed her partialities and prejudices to be seen. This, it is true, could at first be done only in petty matters—invitations withheld from one rival, or visits paid to another; but such indications are significant at a court, and they were not wanting. Mr. Gladstone was left out from state banquets at Windsor, and the Queen lunched with Lord Beaconsfield at his country house—an honor she had paid no minister for years. These very demonstrations of the royal preference, however, contributed to the downfall of the Beaconsfield government; for they were felt to indicate a political bias in Her Majesty, and the idea became prevalent that the court was interfering in politics beyond any recent precedent. The indignation which this belief aroused was in many quarters profound. For a time it seemed as if the monarchical principle had received a blow; no one thought a fatal one, but when a structure stands in any way insecure, when similar ones are tottering or falling on every side, when there are foes within as well as without the walls, the garrison should beware of inviting attack or exposing the vulnerable points, which may thus far have been screened. Immediately after the appearance of the royal book, which was in reality a manifesto, Lord Beaconsfield was hurled from power, and there can be no doubt that the avowed favor of the Crown contributed directly to this result. The people were determined that the Queen should reign, but not rule. The engineer was hoist with his own petard.

The royal feeling at this juncture rose so high that, when the Tories were overthrown, and the time came, according to English usage, for the sovereign to send for the chief of the Opposition to form a government, Her Majesty offered the premiership to two members of the Liberal party before she consented to call Mr. Gladstone to her counsels. But Lord Granville and Lord Hartington were loyal to their chief, and informed the Queen that only Mr. Gladstone would be accepted by the nation; and Her Majesty was obliged to yield, though not, it is said, without tears. So the man she disliked was summoned; he kissed her hand, and became her chief counsellor, the head of her government and the director of all her public acts. The bubble that Lord Beaconsfield had blown so high had burst forever.

The Queen, however, is not without sagacity, and certainly has no wish to imperil her throne. She can discern the line which she must never transgress. She means, besides, to be constitutional, though, if she be so, no English sovereign ever was before; no other was compelled to submit his own will so absolutely and constantly to that of the nation. But the English Constitution grows and changes continuously, like the character of a living man; and the idea of the subjection of the sovereign has developed marvellously of late. Her Majesty is well aware of the tacit conditions on which she keeps her throne, and invariably accepts the situation when it becomes inevitable. So she wiped her eyes. Beaconsfield, the tempter, had led her astray, put naughty notions into her head, and she, not unnaturally, regretted the minister who had flattered her vanity and humored her pride; who added to her titles and pretended to add to her power; but when he was gone, she subsided into the good Queen of present England again—sent telegrams of condolence to sick or dying friends, distributed India shawls among the aristocracy, wrote a book about John Brown instead of the Prince Consort, and for a while let politics alone. She and Mr. Gladstone appeared to rub along very amicably together. The new Prime Minister was asked to the next royal wedding, though when he stayed at Windsor it was said that his sleep was disturbed by the screaming of Beaconsfield's peacocks, which the Queen had brought from her former Premier's funeral.

The English are good-natured, on the whole, and they like dignities and establishments—" something to kotow to;" and Whigs, and even Radicals, content with the possession of place and power, quickly forgot their recent rage. No more diatribes or pamphlets appeared, transcending etiquette and censuring majesty, and the Queen seemed to recover her pristine popularity. It was a family quarrel, after all, and apparently entirely healed; but it would be wiser and better for all concerned not to provoke it again.

## IX.

## THE PERSONAL CHARACTER OF THE QUEEN.

The portrait of the Queen would be incomplete without some recognition of the fact that the personal virtues of Her Majesty have contributed to the stability of the English throne. In this era of revolutions, when Europe is crowded with exiled sovereigns, when Sultans and Czars, and even Presidents, are assassinated, when France and Spain and Rome and Naples and a host of pettier States have not only overthrown their monarchs, but changed the very forms of their governments, the British dynasty has remained undisturbed. Doubtless, this is due in a great measure to the freedom of British institutions as well as to the preference of the British people for whatever is established; but the invariable private excellencies of the Queen have also been conspicuous agents in producing the result.

No breath of scandal has ever lighted on Victoria's fame as wife or widow, and the purity of the atmosphere which she had to create for her court is known to the world. Neither is her beautiful domestic life, preserved amid ceremonies and distractions innumerable and unavoidable, a mere matter of course. The spectacle of other sovereigns of her own age and sex and time demonstrates this. Divided families, rebellious or rival relatives, disobedient children, unfaithful consorts of royal rank abound to-day, as in all history. But Her Majesty, with an absolute confidence in the affection of her subjects, and an instinctive sympathy with the domestic feeling of the British people, has revealed much of her character and daily life in the "Leaves from the Journal of Our Life in the Highlands," and the "Life of the Prince Consort," to which she so largely contributed. Apart from the political character unwisely given to portions of the latter work, there is little in any of these volumes that does not elevate one's idea of the lady who has been able to retain so much simplicity and genuine feeling, amid the pageantries of a palace and the punctilio of a court.

There is doubtless a little of what, to an American and a democrat, seems over-consciousness of rank, a certainty that the most trivial matters concerning herself and her family must be interesting; and the over-weening regard for etiquette, which is one of Her Majesty's most distinctive traits, is often so apparent as to become amusing. She notes how people sit at dinner or the order in which they enter a room as carefully as if these were questions of peace or war, and records the long lists of her guests at weddings or funerals—the only occasions at which she now entertains in state—as gravely as if she were proclaiming treaties or dividing empires. But these peculiarities are perhaps inseparable from her position, and originate in the life she must lead rather than in her individual character or preferences.

On the other hand, the Queen of England exhibits in her exalted sphere virtues which the humblest man or woman in her realm might imitate, virtues which endear her personally to her subjects and certainly make them unwilling in her time to disturb her throne. Purity, honor, truth, religion, fidelity in all the family relations, constancy to friends, sympathy with all forms of human suffering in whatever class—these are traits on account of which the English people of to-day is content to have a Queen.

There may be times when the traits of the woman seem incongruous with the character of a ruler; when the unconscious disposition to submit to another mind, the susceptibility to the influence of a masculine nature, makes the Salique law comprehensible, if not regrettable. Not every favorite or director of the Queen has been a Prince Consort. Beaconsfield and John Brown each exercised a sway that was neither admirable nor beneficial. But there is the other side of the picture, too, and the very womanliness of the Queen has in many ways commended her to her own subjects, while it extorts a sympathetic interest from the world at large. That womanliness makes the country to her no abstraction, but a personality. She feels toward her people as a mother toward her children. There may be to a republican something odd or almost ludicrous in the idea, but there is something touching, and even elevated, besides. The Queen, it is plain, has a downright affection for her people, as for an individual, and, to a certain degree, the affection is returned.

It may be fortunate for the dynasty after all that the sovereign of England in these days is a woman. A very important man once said to me: "This people would not stand another George IV.;" and I have heard court ladies declare they would never kiss the hand of the Prince of Wales. The homage paid the Queen has something in it of the courtesy offered to a lady, and no man is humiliated by kneeling to a woman. We all do that, democrats or not, at some time in our lives.

Even the petty revelations in Her Majesty's latest volume, the very babble about the servants and the family, make a picture of home life and of a garrulous old lady under her crown, that has a certain attraction for the English nature. Her love of country life, her visits to the sick, her gossip with the gillies, her presence at servants' balls—though she never attends an entertainment of the aristocracy—all betray the homespun tastes and virtues of a "gude wife," for all the ermine.

In fact, Her Majesty's sympathies are with the middle class rather than with the aristocracy. She looks like one of them, and, so far as she can, she lives like one of them. I saw her once in public refuse to be cloaked by a duke and turn her shoulders to John Brown. Doubtless Brown performed the service more skilfully, but there was a significance in the act all the same. Her very regard for etiquette, in a lower rank would be the interest of a shop-woman in her wares. I asked General Grant how he was impressed by Her Majesty when he dined at Windsor. He said that when talking with him the Queen had a fidgetty, embarrassed manner, like that of a person unused to her position, but anxious to put him at his ease. She probably wished to show him that she was his superior, and yet to do it in a high-bred way; for in his case she may have had a suspicion that the superiority was not recognized. The sensation must have been unusual.

The people like such stories about her as this. Once upon a time there was a domestic quarrel between the royal pair, and the Prince Consort locked himself in his bedchamber. But soon Her Majesty repented and knocked at the Prince's door. "Who is there?" he asked. "The Queen," was the reply, and no answer came. After a while there was another knock, and again the Prince Consort asked, "Who is there?" "Victoria, Albert," and the door was opened and the quarrel past.

The counterpart to this is the plaintive utterance of Her Majesty on the death of the Prince: "There is no one left to call me Victoria now."

The Queen is, indeed, debarred from ordinary intimacies, and therefore takes her subjects into her confidence. There is the necessity to unbend to some one, and as no one is near enough or grand enough, she unbends to them all, just as she courtesies to a multitude, but never to an individual. Her subjects respect the confidence. Her weaknesses she may betray, but it is to friends. Her eccentricities have been laid bare, but they shall be covered.

The Queen is the granddaughter of George III. in more things than one. She has a touch of his oddity as well as of his obstinacy; she inherits his royal pride and his royal narrowness, but also his idea of duty, his love of country, his fidelity to his family and friends.

I may, perhaps, be permitted to mention the names of two of those friends, not now living, whom many Americans had good reason to esteem, and some to regard with even a kinder feeling. The late Dean of Westminster and his wife, the Lady Augusta Stanley, were both persons of more than ordinary character and admirable qualities, and, while genuinely loyal and attached to British institutions, in no way narrow or prejudiced in their partialities. Both were members of the court for years, and devoted to their royal mistress, and from them I learned many circumstances and traits that made me better appreciate the private character of the Queen. She returned their regard with generous ardor, and has shown that she cherishes their memory still. There must be a charm about her intimate behavior when it attaches natures like theirs.

When the Dean paid his addresses to Lady Augusta Bruce, she was in waiting on Her Majesty, and, immediately after he was accepted, the Queen invited him to dinner. At table she remarked, with a touch of affection in the humor, that she had always thought the Dean of Westminster too faithful a subject to suspect him of enticing away a favorite servant of the Crown. But Lady Augusta retained her connection with the court even after her marriage; she was extra-woman of the bedchamber, as it is called, and was often summoned by her royal mistress for companionship as well as attendance. The Dean was sent to St. Petersburg to perform the English service at the marriage of the Duke of Edinburgh, and his wife accompanied him. In the rigors of a Russian winter the seeds were sown of the lingering and torturing malady that carried her off. While she lay suffering at the Deanery at Westminster, the Queen and the Princesses paid her frequent visits, prayed with her, read with her, wept over her; and in Westminster Abbey there is placed a memorial stone with an inscription indicating that the lady who sleeps beneath was the friend of her sovereign.

There is, however, one phase of the fidelity so strongly marked in Her Majesty's character which some of her subjects do not find so admirable. The higher English, as a rule, do not mourn long or bitterly for their dead; they return promptly to the world of business or of pleasure, and seem easily comforted for the loss of their nearest relatives. They therefore naturally disapprove the Queen's prolonged withdrawal from public life and court entertainments. They miss the pomp which should surround the head of the State on great occasions, as well as the satisfaction of being seen in public with her; while as politicians they deem her seclusion unwise, as perhaps it is. The sentiment of loyalty in our day requires every opportunity of expression or development. It is a plant that does not thrive so well in the shade, and the populace must see Majesty continually in the flesh if it is expected continually to revere. The London tradesmen also murmur at the decreased expenditure of an absent court, which they do not hesitate to attribute to parsimony.

It may, indeed, be true that the Queen should sacrifice her private feeling for a public duty; that she should relax her saddened features and put aside her sombre garb; yet who that has read the most touching portions of her recent volumes but will feel for the wife, so many years a widow, and still constant to the memory of her husband? Who can fail to appreciate the fidelity to the past which can find no pleasure in the present, the grief which in any rank is so rare? To the common people at least this steadfastness of sorrow is pathetic, and certainly in history the figure of this mourning Queen will be as interesting as that of any of the frivolous and beautiful sovereigns whose misfortunes have moved the world. Not Marie Antoinette, nor Josephine, nor the unhappy wandering Eugénie of our own day, appeals for a more tender sympathy than Victoria, seated alone for so many years on so lofty and sad an eminence, not frantic nor rebellious in her sorrow, but faithful, secluded, expectant.

In the gallery of the Queen's private apartments at Windsor there stands a piece of statuary, of life size and nobly conceived, representing the Prince Consort drawn by angels heavenward from the arms of the weeping Queen; beneath is inscribed the line:

"Allured to brighter worlds, and led the way."

To come upon this group amid the splendors of a palace is to feel how completely it expresses the emotion of one who mourns before the nations and is lonely upon a throne.

## X.

### PRECEDENCE IN THE SERVANTS' HALL.

The question of precedence agitates bosoms lower than those of the lords. The rivalries rage in the servants' hall on this account as fiercely as at court. In great houses the servants go in to dinner according to rank, and when the master is entertaining company for a week the butler has a difficult task to arrange the visiting menials in the order of their degrees. First of all is the grand distinction between upper and lower servants—about equivalent to that between lords and commoners, if, indeed, the line is not still more strictly drawn, for lords do dine with commoners, while upper and lower servants may not eat together except during part of the dinner. The butler, the housekeeper, the groom of the chambers, the valets, and the ladies' maids—these constitute the upper classes, and take their meals in the housekeeper's room; the others eat in the servants' hall. At dinner, however, they all sit together, the butler presiding, until the meats have been served; but before the sweets come on, the butler rises, proposes the health of "my lord and lady," all standing; and then the upper servants march solemnly off, according to degree, to the housekeeper's room. They never take their sweets in the servants' hall. Up to this point extreme decorum has been observed, but when the restraint of the imposing presence has been withdrawn greater hilarity prevails below the salt. The footmen begin to flirt with the housemaids, and the grooms and helpers betray that they come from the stables or the yard.

In a great house thirty or forty servants is no unusual number, and when there is a house party as many as a hundred are often assembled, for each guest brings his own servant, and the various valets and maids, the extra coachmen and grooms, make up a company that rivals the array in the drawing-room for pretension and pride. For all these—especially the upper servants—must be placed according to the rank of their masters. The servant of a duke, of course, precedes the servant of an earl, and the valet of an ambassador naturally goes before the gentleman of a mere envoy. They are usually called by the names of their masters, so as to settle at once this point of precedence.

I was once staying at a little inn near Tintern Abbey that I used to frequent, when a coach and four drove up with a party of people who stopped for beer. It was a stately establishment, with liveries and horses all very smart, and I could hear the occupants address each other as "Lady Kitty" and "Sir George," and even "Your Grace" and "Your Excellency." I was new in England then, and looked out of my window to survey the aristocrats. They struck me as rather gay in their dress and not so subdued in manner as those I had met in society, and when the coach drove off I asked the landlord who they were. "Oh," he replied, "they are the servants at the Duke of Beaufort's, who lives near here. He has lent them one of his coaches for a holiday."

I asked my own valet about this fashion of names, and he assured me it was common for servants to call each other in this way. Not long afterward I was visiting at a country-house, where one afternoon the gentlemen went for a walk. I wanted my hat or my cane, and asked the groom of the chambers to call my man. As he went off I stood waiting at the door and heard him calling my own name through the corridor to summon my man.

I learned a lesson about my own degree at Powderham Castle, the seat of the Earl of Devon. I was a Secretary of Legation at the time, and was visiting the house with Mr. Motley, then the American Minister, and my man came to me in great dudgeon one day to complain. Mr. Motley's valet, he said, had introduced him in the servants' hall as "our Secretary's servant."

This man of mine took his own dress-coat when we

went visiting, as regularly as he took mine. All the upper men-servants, he said, were expected to wear dress-coats to dinner, and in some houses the ladies' maids wore low-bodied gowns and gloves. I did not believe him, and asked a friend of mine, the daughter of a marquis, and herself the head of a great establishment. She told me she did not approve the custom, and would not countenance it with her own servants; but that there were ducal houses in which an allowance was made to the ladies' maids and the housekeepers for gloves to wear to dinner.

This recalls a story about the Queen. Her Majesty once observed that one of her maids of honor wore soiled gloves, and was told that the lady was poor and could not afford fresh gloves every time she went on duty—at least on four hundred pounds a year. Thereupon the Queen added to the lady's stipend, with the express understanding that the gloves were to be renewed for every occasion of ceremony. Thus superiors regard the incomes of their attendants as well as their own state, all the way up and down the scale.

For the Queen doubtless looks upon her servants as a duchess does upon hers; unless, indeed, the distance between the Queen and a duchess is greater than that between the duchess and her maid. At the time of the engagement of the Princess Louise a story was current which shows what the high

English believe to be the feeling of the Queen. In the royal establishment there is a separate table for the household, at which even the minister in attendance eats when he is not invited to the Queen's. According to gossip, Lord Lorne went to lunch with his future wife, and was asked to the table of Her Majesty. His mother, the Duchess of Argyll, was mistress of the robes, and when he entered the Queen's dining-room, Lord Lorne asked: "Where is the Duchess?" "Oh! she is lunching with the household."

But to return to the servants' hall. When I went to Dunrobin with General Grant, it was convenient for me to take a footman, and General Grant had a courier. Now, a footman in livery is not an upper servant, but, unmindful of this important regulation, I had put my man into plain clothes. In consequence, he was supposed to be a valet, and was admitted to the august society of the housekeeper's room. All went well in the borrowed state till he quarrelled with the courier, who then revealed that James was a mere liveried servant, and the poor fellow was relegated to the hall. It was worse than being degraded from the diplomatic corps to the general circle at court.

I was staying once at a house where there had been a grand quarrel between the maids of Lady Torrington and Lady Molesworth. Lord Torrington was a viscount and Lady Molesworth only the widow of a baronet. But the Torringtons were poor and Lady Molesworth was very rich; it was said that Lord Torrington managed her estates for her. Upon this her Abigail presumed, vainly supposing with the pride of wealth that her mistress was superior in consequence to those who belonged to the peerage. She was absolutely about to take precedence as they went in to dinner. But Lady Torrington's maid haughtily thrust her back, and exclaimed: "You are only the servant of a baronet's widow, and my mistress is the wife of the Right Honorable Viscount Torrington, Lord in Waiting to Her Majesty." Of course the superior claim was allowed, and Lady Molesworth's maid remained behind in merited confusion. The story reached the upper regions, where it created a deal of laughter, but no one seemed to suppose it reflected any ridicule on real rank. The distinctions in the drawing-room are important; only those in the servants' hall are trivial.

Lord Derby was a visitor at this same house, a castle in the Highlands, and when he was about to leave, his valet was toasted at dinner. The statesman is quiet and reserved in the last degree, dislikes parade, and avoids speeches whenever it is possible. So when the Earl of Derby's name was "mentioned" in the hall, his man arose, put both hands on the table after the fashion of the Earl, bowed first to the right and then to the left, and sat down without saying a word. The fellow had borrowed his master's manner as well as his name. How the report of this incident reached the host I cannot say, but he told it to me.

I once went to a wedding breakfast in the servants' hall. It was at a house in Wales. The bride had been the nursery maid of one of the children, and the bridegroom was a young farmer on the estate; for in England domestic service is not considered degrading. The farmers and small tradesmen are on a level with the ordinary servants in a great house, and quite look up to the housekeeper and the butler. They all say "sir" and "ma'am" to these great personages just as the nobility do to the Princes and the Queen.

Even persons of consideration in the middle class associate with the servants of the higher aristocracy. Some years ago I was visiting at a house near one of the most important towns in middle England, and went into the town to consult a doctor. He was an accomplished man, and I had an extremely interesting conversation with him. When I left he said I needed further treatment, and asked me where he should call. I answered, "At Bretton Park." "What!" he exclaimed. "Are you stopping there? Why, I visit their butler." The awe with which he regarded a guest at Bretton was amusing.

I had another acquaintance whom I highly

esteemed, a very respectable Englishman, who belonged to the middle class. I was once telling him of a visit I had paid to a Yorkshire nobleman, and he said he knew the butler well; he often went to see him, and the butler always got out some very choice port, for my friend was a judge of wine. One day when he was praising the brand the butler exclaimed: "What would his lordship give for a bottle of this wine?" I always wanted to tell this story to *my* host, but I thought it would be a breach of confidence toward the butler.

But the wedding waits all this while. The family was Catholic, but they were Squires of the parish all the same, and had their pew in the parish church, though they never went to service. Mass was said for them in a private chapel in the house. This morning, however, the young ladies went to the marriage, and took me with them as a guest. The pew was in the chancel, within the altar rails, and we had a good view of the bride. The village girls strewed flowers in her way, and she was buxom and as blushing as if of higher degree. After the ceremony the young squire, a lad of seventeen, invited me to the breakfast. There was an Italian baron also on a visit at the house, and the occasion was as curious to him as to the American democrat; so he accompanied us.

The servants were about forty in number, and sat at a table shaped like an L, the upper servants, of course, at the upper end, and the others below the corner. When we entered they all rose and remained standing while the young squire toasted the bride. The baron and I drank her health in some very good sherry which the servants were allowed for the occasion. The youngster spoke of the regret he felt in losing a faithful servant of his house; at this the little boy, whose nurse she had been, and who sat next her at table, put his arm around the bride, and she whimpered, and so did the housemaids all down the line, and the bridegroom looked as if he thought this wasn't fair. But the heir, with great tact for one so young, and an Englishman, too, hastened to say that, since she was to leave them, it was pleasant to think she had become the wife of one of their own farmers, known to them for his honesty, and so forth, and so on. Then the bridegroom blushed, and everybody was satisfied. As we were leaving the room the procession of upper servants started off in state, but I saw my poor James, who had once been allowed to accompany them, remaining behind in his livery.

Afterward we had our luncheon, and then there was a dance on the lawn; and the ladies, the baron, and I were there to see. There was a blind harper, for it was Wales, and the dance was Sir Roger de Coverley, which, for those who may need the information, I will say is the same with the Virginia reel. The bridegroom led off with one of the daughters of the house, the young squire took out the bride, and the baron and I had our pick of the housemaids for partners; and mine was as rosy and pretty an English girl as ever I danced with at court.

## XI.

## THE HOUSE OF LORDS.

In all social matters the aristocracy retains its old supremacy, but in politics the sceptre has departed from Judah. Up to the time of the passage of the Reform bill in 1832 the political influence of the peers was paramount; but since that epoch it has waned. The nobility, it is true, like the Queen, still wears the insignia of power, but the only use of the coronet now is to put it on the coffin. The House of Lords, it is true, is one of the estates of the realm; its assent is nominally indispensable to the validity of every law; but both Crown and peers are dragged at the chariot wheels of the Commons. The Lords make a good fight; they die hard, but their political decadence is undoubted. The most august assemblage in Europe, as Britons like to call the House of Lords, is only a body to register the decrees of the Lower Chamber; and if it dares dispute the will of the Prime Minister or the Commons, it is threatened with an invasion of new members, to which the irruptions of the barbarians into the Roman Senate or the Parisian mob into the various

French assemblies were antecedents and parallels. These ancient and foreign assaults preceded revolution, and the British aristocrats know the signs, and yield.

Ever since the memorable battle between William IV. and his ministers, in 1832, and the determination of Lord Grey to create peers in sufficient numbers to carry the Reform bill, the House of Lords has recognized its subordinate position. After repeated struggles, after rejecting the bill again and again, after dissolutions of Parliament and changes of the ministry, after general elections, which triumphantly supported the measure for extending representation, the Lords were still obstinate. The King was on their side, but the people were determined, and, for the second time in English history, King and Lords found themselves weaker than the Commons. Charles I. was the principal personage in the contest of his day, and the nobility stood behind him; two hundred years later it was the Lords who led the defence, while the King was in the background, although an ardent ally. At last the Prime Minister, himself an earl, advised the King to create a sufficient number of peers to turn the scale, but the King refused. Thereupon the Ministry resigned, and the Duke of Wellington undertook to form a new Government and stem the tide. But he also proved powerless. The former ministry returned, and William IV. made his submission in these words: "The King grants permission to Earl Grey and to his Chancellor, Lord Brougham, to create such a number of peers as will be sufficient to insure the passing of the Reform bill." Upon this, rather than be overwhelmed by the new creations, a majority of the Opposition absented themselves from the House of Lords, and the bill was passed. It was known then that the aristocracy of England would never again be able seriously to withstand the will of the people. The knell of their political power had sounded.

They retain, nevertheless, all their conservative instincts, and rally round a sinking cause with a devotion which one cannot but admire. *Noblesse oblige*, and the latest additions, the grandsons of barbers and tailors, are as inflexible in their loyalty to their order as those descended from the Plantagenets. Even Mr. Gladstone's creations desert him on the first opportunity; the very colleagues of his cabinet, the Radicals of the Radicals, go over to the enemy when once they get within the precincts and the influence of the House of Lords. For the peers vote in solid phalanx; perhaps too solidly or stolidly. They cannot see that sometimes to yield a little would be to save a little. Their instinct is to defend every outwork, to repel every assault.

But it is only when their rank or their retroactive policy is in danger that they pay much attention to politics. Shorn of their ancient influence, they probably dislike to be constantly reminded of their insignificance, and are apparently indifferent to the ordinary course of public affairs. Some of this indifference, it is true, may proceed from senility. Of those who attend the House of Lords one-fifth have passed the age of threescore and ten, thirty-seven are upward of seventy five, and twenty-three are octogenarians. The average age of a peer is fifty-eight. Bouvier defines senility to be "a loss of energy in some of the intellectual operations, while the affections remain natural and unperverted." This exactly describes the condition of the ancient peers, if not of the entire venerable body, whose affections still cling to their former consequence, though their intellect and energy are insufficient to retain it.

But incapacity as much as decrepitude is responsible for the apathy of the Lords. The ability of the peerage is for the most part confined to the men who have forced their way into it. Out of twenty-eight dukes only one has shown marked political intelligence, and he would hardly have attracted attention had he been born in a lower degree. Of all the other nobles long descended Lord Derby and Lord Salisbury only are prominent, and these cognate statesmen themselves can hardly be called men of genius. Clever men, it is true, do not abound in any class of life, and Diogenes needed his lamp on the outside of the House of Lords; but the peers are the *aristoi*, the best; the legislators for a nation. They have every advantage of education, association with the ablest, early and wide experience of affairs, the habit of authority, the confidence of their equals, the deference of the mass; yet the body is not even second rate in business capacity or political tact, to say nothing of intellectual acquirement or power. The peers enjoy but do not employ their splendid opportunities. The younger ones make no pretence of fitting themselves for their functions. I knew, indeed, one eldest son of an earl who went as a clerk in a government office, to learn government business, but I never heard of another, and he soon grew tired of the drudgery and returned to his yacht and his drag. The cadets of great houses sometimes devote themselves to politics, but the heirs can dispense with the effort, for they will be peers all the same.

Even the additions to the peerage seldom display ability after they enter the charmed portals. Sir Stafford Northcote and Mr. Lowe were both considered shelved when they were turned into peers. Their promotion was their greatest defeat. The House of Lords was called the Hospital for Incurables in Horace Walpole's time. What would he have christened it to-day?

Besides all this, it is a notable fact that genius, though it may be ennobled, is rarely transmitted. It is the title, not the talent, that is hereditary. No descendant of a Lord Chancellor has ever rivalled his ancestor, and of all the successors of those whose ability raised them to the House of Lords, only one is famous to-day. Instead of fostering or developing talent, rank seems to have a crushing or withering influence, and the aristocracy is decidedly less brilliant since it has been extended.

Under these circumstances the peers are wise, perhaps, to accept the situation. How should they fight when they have no weapons? In 1878 there were only four divisions, as the formal votings are called, in the House of Lords, and these were on questions of minor importance. In 1879, when the foreign policy of the Government was at stake, only about half of the peers could be found to attend four divisions. Thirty-five peers were absent altogether from 1875 to 1880. In 1877 it was considered remarkable that the average attendance of peers was close upon one hundred during the fifty-two sittings before Easter, and there are six hundred members of the House. In 1881 their admirers boasted that "about one hundred and thirty peers address the House each session, and half the debates go on until close upon the dinner hour!" which is eight o'clock. The Lords meet at five.

It is seldom indeed that the state of the country detains the hereditary legislator from his evening meal. Dinner parties in London are made with reference to the hours of the House of Commons, which does not sit on Wednesdays or Saturdays, and there are five invitations for those evenings to one for any other. But you can catch your lord for any night; he is never prevented by public business—at least, not three times in a session.

An ordinary sitting of the House of Lords is a dull and dreary ceremony. The hall is lofty, and in the dim light of an English afternoon reminds one of some stately vault where the remains of the ancestral institution may be imagined to repose. A few straggling gentlemen are seated on the benches, some mumbling remarks are made, some antiquated form gone through in the darkness—a new peer is perhaps presented in his robes, or a bill comes up from the Commons—and the august assembly adjourns. The business of the House is carried on by thirty or forty peers, and these, with rare exceptions, maintain the debates of the session. The uniformity of costume is broken only by the Lord Chancellor as he enters or leaves with his robes and his train-bearer, or the ghostly bishops who sit on benches by themselves, in their lawn sleeves. The mover and seconder of an address that is offered to the Queen at the opening of every session are always in levee dress—for they are supposed to stand in the presence of Majesty, though Majesty never is there—but otherwise the peers are plainly clad, the older ones, as a rule, unfashionably, and more than half of them wear their hats. All is dismal, decorous, and funereal.

I have, however, seen the chamber filled in every seat, and the peeresses' gallery crowded. When an opportunity occurs to signify their opposition to a liberal measure the Lords turn out in force, and if, as once in a very great while happens, the sitting is late, the wives and daughters of peers come in from dinner in laces and diamonds, while the peers themselves on these occasions are often in evening dress on the floor. After some bill to which their lordships are opposed has passed the House of Commons, the patricians proceed to set forth their arguments elaborately, and sometimes violently. I have been present at as heated discussions in the aristocratic chamber as ever I witnessed in the American Capitol.

When the bill to disestablish the Irish Church was debated, the Prime Minister, Mr. Gladstone, stood on the steps of the throne in an excited House while Lord Salisbury denounced him in terms as an "arrogant man," and every one turned to see how he took it. For there is no admission to the floor of the House for ministers who are not peers. Privy Councillors, the eldest sons of peers, and members of the diplomatic corps may stand on the steps of the throne; and, if the session is long and they become fatigued, these personages often sit or squat in extremely undignified postures behind the railings that surround the sovereign's seat. In this way the Prime Minister who had created thirty or forty peers in his time, and could have doubled the number had he chosen, had no seat in the aristocratic presence, and remained standing while he was berated by a member of the nobility.

Not only individuals, but the Commons themselves, the coördinate branch of the Legislature, have no place assigned them in the Upper Chamber, except at the entrance and below the bar; a relic this of the ancient arrogance with which the representatives of the people were treated by the peers. Even when the Commons are summoned to hear the reading of a speech or message from the throne, no seats are allowed them; they rush in from their own House, pell-mell and headlong, like a parcel of schoolboys, to secure a place as near as possible to the bar which divides them from the nobility.

On the night I speak of Dean Stanley was on the steps of the throne by favor, for he had many friends among the ushers, and "black rods," as well as among the Lords. He took me in to dine with him at the deanery, which is close to the Parliament houses. One of the Irish archbishops whose fate was at stake accompanied us, for the debate was closing and a division was imminent, and nobody wished to go far to dinner. The Dean was an intimate friend of the prelate, and said to me sadly that this might be the last occasion when the archbishop would sit in the House of Lords. It was like dining with a man before his execution. But the archbishop was brave and talked on indifferent topics with the American democrat.

That night members who rarely or never set foot in the House of Lords were present in scores, but at ordinary divisions the number who vote, small as it is compared with the aggregate of the peers, is collected only by the energetic pressure of the politician called the "whip," because he whips the noblemen in. The peers seem to value their privilege principally as a means of asserting their opinions when these are opposed to the policy certain in the end to prevail.

While I was in England the Lords, as a body, resisted every step in the direction of progress or reform. They opposed the ballot, the educational system now in force, the disestablishment of the Irish Church, the abolition of purchase in the army, and every measure calculated to extend the suffrage, to favor the sale of land, or to modify the condition of Ireland; yet in every case they were obliged to yield. Not long ago Mr. Gladstone declared: "Only for fifteen years of the last fifty has the ministry of the day possessed the confidence of the House of Lords;" that is, only for fifteen years out of fifty has the House of Lords been in harmony with the Government which represented the judgment and will of the people of England.

If all modern ideas are not wrong, if liberalism does not lead, as the peers believe, only to revolution, corruption, and anarchy, the condition of England has improved since the overthrow of the Lords. By their fruits ye shall know them. The catalogue of reforms which they have opposed proves not only their impotence in actual politics, but the unfavorable nature of such influence as they still retain. This is shown not only negatively by what they have been unable to accomplish, but by the prosperity of the country without them or in spite of them. Since political power has passed into other hands the population of England has doubled, its wealth has quintupled, its commerce has extended beyond comparison, its manufactures have crowded the shops and warehouses of the world. The material comfort of the people of every class has been marvellously increased, education has been more widely diffused, and whatever goes to make up the prosperity and happiness of a nation has been furthered and promoted since the downfall of the Lords.

Newspapers in their present stage of development, navigation by steam, railroads, telegraphs, the various and extended uses of electricity—all have come into existence under the new order of things; all are the inventions or improvements of the middle class; all are the natural and legitimate result of the great measures which the House of

Lords resisted. Meanwhile, the grandeur of the empire is in no way diminished; the influence of England is as potent as in any previous era; her boundaries are widened; in Africa and Asia she stretches out her territories. But her best soldiers are not the sons of lords; her lawyers spring from the middle, or even the lower, class; her merchant princes may not be presented at court; her men of letters and science and art are not aristocrats; her greatest Prime Minister for a generation refuses to be a peer.

## XII.

### THE PRINCESS OF WALES.

It is sixteen years since I was presented to the Princess of Wales. The beauty of the royal Dane was then in all its freshness, and I was struck with the stately presence, the speaking eye, the winning smile, the appearance of intelligence, as well as by the affability of manner, which at that time was marked, but has not always been so conspicuous since. The long succession of salutations and ceremonies, the ever-recurring necessity for graciousness probably becomes irksome at times. I once heard a court lady say that there is always something of the pump-handle in royal civilities. But, if wearisome to dispense, they are often refreshing to the recipient.

The Princess is more like a princess in appearance and bearing than any other I have seen; far transcending her higher-born sisters-in-law, the daughters of the Queen and the Duchess of Edinburgh; and quite equal to any princess of the stage or the story-books. Yet she was born the daughter of an obscure half-German duke, without a probability of ever becoming royal. Ten years after she came into the world it was agreed by the great powers of Europe that her father should be King in Denmark, on the death of the sovereign then reigning; and he still had not arrived at this dignity when Alexandra was sought and won by the heir to the English throne. Denmark itself is no great things in the way of a kingdom, but Sleswig-Holstein-Sonderbourg-Glücksbourg, the paternal duchy of the future Queen-consort of England, was still more inconsiderable. Her mother and grandmother were both petty princesses of Hesse-Cassel, the same insignificant little State whose soldiers were sold to England, to fight us in our Revolutionary war, so that blood can hardly be said to tell in her case. It is not inherited grandeur that gives the princely air. After the heavy German procreators had done their part, the fairies must have brought their gifts to the cradle.

This world is very much given to malice, and high-bred English dames are not always exempt from the failing. The Princess is invariably well dressed; and when I once said so, a great lady replied: "She learned how to dress when she made her own bonnets and gowns, on a hundred a year, before her father was King of Denmark." It was, indeed, a strange fortune that raised the daughters of Christian IX. to two of the proudest positions in Christendom. One is already Empress of All the Russias, and the other is mated to the man who may, one day, be sovereign of England. Such matches have not often been made by portionless maidens. But the heirs apparent to these great monarchies both wanted consorts who were not Catholic; and marriageable princesses answering the demand were scarce when the Czarewitch and the Prince of Wales arrived at their majorities. The sons of sovereigns, however, may not wait long to be wived, for the succession must be settled; so the two ladies stepped from their obscurity in Copenhagen up to the pinnacle of human grandeur, outranking and overtopping the daughters of the very potentates who had made their father royal. They would, doubtless, at one time have thought themselves honored to bear the trains of some who are now, or may yet be, their subjects.

The family affection of these fortunate sisters is strong. They cherish the recollection of their early home life, and like to go back to little Denmark with their children and spouses and throw aside for a while the trappings and restraints of their more recent splendor; for in Copenhagen the King and Queen live in great simplicity. I was once offered the post of Minister to the Danish court, and informed myself as to its ways. The diplomatic corps, I was told, and the high nobility call and take tea with the royal family of an afternoon. The revenues are so small, that the life at the palace is necessarily plain.

The Czarevna visited the Princess of Wales, while her husband was still Czarewitch, and they made a sightly picture as they drove about London together in a low, open carriage. They look alike, though the Princess is the prettier and by far the more elegant. The English common people like to see the family feeling respected by the highest, and the belief that their future Queen is a good sister and daughter, as well as wife and mother, adds to her hold on them.

That hold is certainly strong. No member of the royal family is more popular with the country at large; perhaps none is so popular. The people, of course, never see her, except in public; but daily, in the "season," they assemble at the gate of Marlborough House, when it is known that she is to drive; and I doubt if among all who penetrate those portals the Princess has warmer admirers than in the congregation that waits on the outside. They like to see the royal children in her company, and the Princess often takes her daughters with her; sometimes, doubtless, to gratify the commonalty as well as herself and her family. She dresses them plainly; their hats and frocks are not so smart by half as those of many of the children of wealthy Londoners who may never go to court.

At one time there were stories of infidelity on the part of the Prince of Wales, and a sort of sympathy was aroused for the wife who, it was fancied, was neglected; but the Princess always behaved with dignity. If she thought she had wrongs, she betrayed neither resentment nor jealousy to the world, and at last it became a question whether any dissatisfaction had ever existed on her part—a triumph of discretion and decorum not often surpassed.

When the Prince was ill she watched over him with every demonstration of devotion, and was as delighted as the happiest of wives when at last he began to mend. But, alas for poor human nature! her anxiety can hardly be regarded as evidence of affection, for she would never have been Queen of England had her husband died. Had he been the most unfaithful of mankind she would doubtless have prayed just as hard for his recovery.

At this crisis she received the greatest possible proof of her popularity. She was universally admitted to be the proper person to be named for Regent in case the Prince should die. The next heir to the throne must then have had a long minority, and it was indispensable to consider the contingency of the death of the Queen. The question was not long in doubt. A few words were said here and there for the Duke of Edinburgh, but in every circle and class, not only among the people of rank and political power who were to decide, but in the press and with the country at large, one wish and one opinion prevailed: in the event of the need of a Regency, the Regent must be the Princess of Wales.

Perhaps in part this was because the Princess has never been credited with ability. She does not lack a certain intelligence, I am told, and shows sufficient interest in the topics that come up at court; but she has never displayed political insight or ambition. She has neither taste nor genius for the political intrigues in which so many princesses take delight, and no anxiety, apparently, to influence political affairs. Had she been placed at the head of the State she would doubtless have done whatever her ministers dictated or desired. The Duke of Edinburgh, on the contrary, is believed to have a will of his own, and a sulky disposition besides, and he might have given trouble. He has never been popular, either in society or with the people at large. So the Princess was easily successful, though she made no effort to secure the prize.

At this juncture both the Queen and the Princess exhibited a pathetic and beautiful bit of womanly feeling that became them better than crown or coronet. One of the young grooms at Sandringham fell ill of the same fever of which the Prince of Wales was believed to be dying, and these royal ladies visited the lad in his room at the stables, sat by his bedside, and displayed, and doubtless felt, a very touching interest in the youth whose pains and peril were the same as those of the heir to mightiest monarchies. The groom, however, died before the Prince was out of danger, and the anxious Queen and her sad daughter-in-law sent their gentlemen to the funeral, while the Princess stood at the window to watch the procession as it bore the body to that dread home which prince and peasant must inhabit at last. Touches of genuine feeling like this endear the Queen to her subjects, and it is the same womanliness in the Princess that makes her popular with those who know her only from afar.

She does not, however, seem to attach very closely those who are about her intimately. I have never heard these speak of her with enthusiasm. The people at court all call her amiable, but nothing more. She is doubtless a woman negative in character as well as in ability. She likes the company of her favorites, but these are never of the very brilliant sort. She enjoys the opera and the theatre, for there she is free from the necessity of dispensing incessant courtesies; but she has no pleasures more intellectual than these. She is not accomplished, beyond speaking several languages, an art in which princes are always supposed to be proficient. She has heard the greatest music and seen the greatest paintings, and knows and to a degree appreciates both music and the pictorial art; but this is all.

Her temper is never unfavorably discussed, and her fame is as unspotted as the Queen's. Her tact is on most occasions sufficient, but never supreme; it never rises into that genius for society and affairs which makes a great woman of the world. On the whole, I should call her wooden; a beautiful, graceful doll, framed to perform her public functions well; but she has hardly any others: her private life is a matter of public knowledge. She makes no enemies and no ardent friends; has no enthusiasms herself, and evokes none in others, except in those who are not close enough to perceive that the automaton is wound up and that the figure has comparatively little heart; perhaps after all the very best sort of person for the place she fills.

She is deaf and lame, but the mass of those who are in her presence discover neither defect. Louis XIV., though below the medium height, is said to have appeared tall to his obsequious courtiers, and so the Princess seems to listen and not to limp. The glamour that royalty throws around her conceals the comparative coldness that lies beneath a graceful exterior, while her intellectual dulness is disguised under the dignified decorums of a court.

The Princess has apparently no personal influence with the Queen. Indeed, although no shadow of a difference has even been apparent or suggested, there is certainly no conspicuous intimacy between these august kinswomen. The Princess rarely visits the Queen at Osborne or Balmoral; the Queen still more rarely goes to Sandringham or Abergeldie, the seats of the Prince of Wales. The name of the Princess does not appear in the last "Leaves from Our Journal in the Highlands," where Her Majesty catalogues all her favorites, from royal relatives down to gillies and collies. The sovereign's own daughters arrange her robes when she opens Parliament, but this graceful duty is never performed by the future Queen.

The Princess, however, often holds drawing-rooms in the absence of Her Majesty. She represents the Queen always at court concerts and balls, and sometimes on still more public occasions. There can, of course, be no question of her rank, and the Queen is too rigid in her regard for etiquette to ignore or neglect what is due to the wife of her heir apparent. The relations between the ladies are all that are required, but in this, as in her other excellencies, the Princess never oversteps the limits of moderation. She possesses, indeed, all the moderate virtues, all the negative qualities desirable in her station; but she has not one tithe of the heart of the Queen, or of the faulty Prince of Wales.

She lives in forms, and naturally thinks much of them. Her personal attendants are required to observe every punctilio. She goes through her own part, and expects them to do the same. The royal yacht was once arriving at Cowes with the Prince and Princess abroad, and an immense concourse awaited them at the landing. But the Princess had been seasick all day, and was not recovered when the Prince himself came to fetch her to meet the multitude. Her ladies assured His Royal Highness that their mistress was unable to stand. But the excuse could not be accepted; the people must not be disappointed; and the Princess was decked in her jewels between the paroxysms of sickness, and, pale and faint, was led out to courtesy and smile to her future subjects.

If etiquette is thus inexorable for the mistress, it is, of course, never relaxed for the maid. A countess whose name is well known in America was in attendance on the Princess at Osborne, when a friend of mine went to call on her. The guest was received in a bedroom, for there was no other place reserved for the ladies-in-waiting, and they could not, of course, entertain their acquaintances in the apartments of royalty. While the two ladies were talking a summons came for the countess. "The Princess was going to bathe." "But, my dear, you do not bathe because the Princess does?" "Certainly I do." "But you are not well; you may be injured." "Ah! my dear, I am in waiting." And, as there was but one room, the visitor was obliged to leave, while the countess dressed to attend the Princess in her bath.

## XIII.

### AMERICAN MINISTERS.

I suppose a man can hardly be American Minister in London without contracting something of the aristocratic feeling. The disease is in the air. Everything fosters the delusion that he belongs to the oligarchy. His precedence is defined; he has his place in every pageant or parade; he is called "His Excellency;" his carriage need not stand in the rank at balls, but drives magnificently by all the lesser nobility, who fall back to let him pass. He even enters the ambassadors' door at court. The sturdiest republican soon gets used to the deference, and comes to think it appropriate as well as agreeable. I heard one of our ministers say he would rather be an English duke than anything else on earth, and another declare that England is the only country in which a gentleman should either live or die. They flatter themselves that their tendencies and tastes are English, but it is aristocratic English only; none of them want to belong to the middle class. Whenever they can, they claim connection with the aristocracy, happy if they can trace a pedigree to some ignoble offshoot of a noble house, which repudiates as often as it admits the consanguinity; or prouder of a descent from a country squire who had a coat of arms than to bear American names that genius has made illustrious.

'Tis strange the effect the contact has. There have been American Ministers at London as punctilious, as exacting, as regardless of courtesy when mere etiquette was in question, as any of their colleagues in the corps. I have known them wear knee-breeches at church when every one else was in plain clothes, and insist on their precedence with all the pertinacity of peeresses or parvenus. There was once a question of the rank of the daughters of diplomatists. Several of the ambassadors and envoys were widowers, and in society their unmarried daughters had long been allowed the precedence accorded to wives. But at last the wives demurred, and the mighty matter was referred to the sovereign. Before the decision came I heard an American Minister say to his wife: "If those girls attempt to pass before you, I order you to push them back." The Queen, however, spoke in time, and there was no necessity for so high-handed a vindication of democratic claims. The daughters of a diplomatist, it was decreed, possess no rank at court. If they have a mother, they follow her; if not, they must attend some other diplomatic matron, of whose suite or family they are supposed, for the occasion, to form a part.

All daughters but her own, indeed, receive rigorous measure from the Queen; and against diplomatic daughters she seems to bear almost a special grudge, refusing them the privileges accorded to daughters whose rank is derived from birth. Perhaps this springs from the English sentiment that official rank is insignificant. Diplomatic precedence is, in royal eyes, the mere fringe of office; not, like inherited precedence, a permanent superiority—the essential and integral appurtenance of rank that is not acquired. English diplomatists themselves lose all their official precedence the moment they set foot in England. Sir Edward Thornton, when he went to court, after representing Her Majesty for years in Washington, was only a knight of recent creation. He did not even belong to the aristocracy, and took his place far down the line—a very worthy person who had risen from the middle class.

Some years ago an American Minister had several daughters living with him, one of whom was a widow. This lady was invited to one court ball with her father and his family, but for the second she received no card. The minister, supposing the omission accidental, sent to the Lord Chamberlain to have it rectified. But the court functionaries explained that the exclusion was designed. One invitation had been sent to the lady out of compliment to her father, but she must not expect to be admitted every time. Having married, she had left her father's family, in the estimation of the Queen. For all these rules are the express determination of the sovereign—the fruit of calm, ripe judgment and profound deliberation on her part.

The American envoys are usually very much disgusted because they are not ambassadors, for many privileges are accorded to these highest potentates of diplomacy that are not conceded to mere ministers. It is ambassadors only who can claim the title of Excellency; to others it is given by courtesy alone. Ambassadors only have a right to demand an interview with the sovereign; and on the few occasions when the Queen still entertains in person and in state, at royal weddings or ceremonial funerals, her diplomatic invitations are restricted to ambassadors and to the representatives of such sovereigns as are connections of her family. This, of course, always excludes the American Minister, who sometimes never goes to Windsor except to present his credentials and his recall. But, more humiliating still, a minister may wait an hour at the Foreign Office for an interview with the Secretary for Foreign Affairs, and at the end of the hour see an ambassador arrive and go in before him. The representatives of the great republic feel that these things should not be; that the dignity of the United

States requires that its diplomatic servants should have equal standing with those of any other power. And it is hard to say that they are wrong. If we maintain a representative at a court where these rules prevail, we should for our own sake insure him proper consideration. The Minister of the United States should not be thrust back because of lower rank by the representative of any petty State that happens to keep an ambassador.

But the ministers sometimes show more feeling on this subject than comports with the station that they fill. One of them begged a British Secretary for Foreign Affairs to address our Government, and request the elevation of the American legation into an embassy. He was so pertinacious in his applications that the Englishman complained of them in society; a fact that did not add to the dignity which the envoy was so anxious to maintain.

I have said that the ministers become punctilious. One of them was dining at an American house, and as he took his hostess down to dinner she asked him if he would consent to sit on her left at table, so that she might arrange her guests, only eight or ten in number, more agreeably. But the inflexible republican replied: "Do you know that I outrank a duke?"—a supererogatory illustration, for their were no dukes at dinner. So the poor little lady's table was disarranged, but the American Minister maintained his place. The worst of it was, he was wrong in his etiquette. By express determination of Her Majesty, foreign envoys follow dukes. But our countryman was new at his post, and doubtless learned his lesson better afterward. If he didn't, the dukes soon told him.

A minister, indeed, must often shudder when he remembers the blunders he has made. One of our representatives on the Continent who later thought himself an authority on ceremonies, in the early days of his exaltation kindly left a card on the King, whereupon His Majesty remarked that he had been told Americans were sometimes unmindful of forms, but this one had paid him an honor he had never before received.

But not every American representative is so absorbed in the sense of his own consequence as to forget or neglect politeness for punctilio. While General Schenck was Minister to England, Mr. Reverdy Johnson, who had held the same position not very long before, was visiting London, and both gentlemen dined with me on the same evening. Before we went in to dinner, General Schenck particularly requested that I would give Mr. Johnson precedence. His predecessor was old, and had, of course, been used to taking the first place, and the General wished to show him deference. This graceful act was prompted by sheer good breeding, not indifference; for I had expected to invite a Cardinal for the same evening, and inquired of General

Schenck about the precedence. He said that, as American Minister, he could not waive his rank in favor of a prelate who, though a prince in the Church of Rome, had no recognized place according to English rules.

Mr. Pierrepont, also, always waived his rank in favor of General Grant, and this was not entirely a work of supererogation. Many Englishmen otherwise would have placed the actual representative of the United States before the ex-President. At a dinner at Kensington Palace, where Lord Lorne was host, he inquired of Mr. Pierrepont, before the guests were arranged, whether he waived his rank in favor of General Grant.

For in the country to which he is accredited, a diplomatic representative takes precedence even of a member of the Government that he serves. Mr. Motley told me that, when he was minister at Vienna, before the days of the German empire, he once had Bismarck and the Prussian ambassador both at dinner. Bismarck was chief of the Foreign Office in Berlin at the time, and the question of precedence was raised, but settled in favor of the ambassador, and Bismarck followed his own subordinate.

All is not happiness at foreign courts. The ministers' families have their own difficulties. They always want to snub the wives of the Secretaries of legation, and the Secretaries' wives, being good

Americans, won't stand the snubbing. I recollect one who offered to matronize the daughter of a widowed minister, and the shock which the proposal created was not surprising to one familiar with the workings of the feminine mind. I think myself the offer was mere bravado. The same lady has since been a minister's wife herself, and I doubt not she made her Secretaries' wives know their place. There are no sticklers for subordination like servants who have passed through the degrees, and no such disciplinarians in the army as officers who have risen from the ranks.

Secretaries of legation, indeed, are a frequent source of trouble. The ministers have not their choice of them, as a rule. They must take whomsoever the Washington officials send. One veteran in etiquette had a Western editor inflicted on him, who went to court without a waistcoat, and, of course, was turned away. And the minister was a Bostonian!

There are other trials still for the luckless representative. I have already described the struggles of Americans determined to go to court. But some of our compatriots are not content with palatial hospitalities; they want invitations to private houses, too, and expect their minister to provide them. One gentleman, not altogether unknown on this side of the Atlantic, after reading the list of private parties printed every Monday in the *Morning Post* to refresh the memory of the aristocrats, cut out the catalogue and enclosed it to the minister, and requested "tickets" for the entire schedule.

But the worst troubles of the ministers are about their clothes. Some years ago, Congress established a rule that the diplomatic representatives of the United States should wear no uniform whatever not prescribed by law. Up to that time, our ministers abroad had worn a suitable enough sort of dress which made them look somewhat like other people at court; not conspicuous by plainness, nor ostentatious from ornament. There was no authority for the custom, but none against it, until some rampant republican declared it unworthy of a State without a King to deck its ministers in foreign frippery, and the law prohibiting diplomatic uniforms was passed.

The envoy at the Court of St. James was informed of the rule, and he, in his turn, notified the English Secretary for Foreign Affairs. An elaborate correspondence thereupon ensued, which was submitted to the Queen herself, and a compromise was finally agreed upon, to the effect that at levees the United States Minister and the members of his legation would be received in ordinary evening dress, but at drawing-rooms and at court balls and concerts they were to wear knee-breeches and swords. This was approved by the Secretary of State for the time being, and has since been the rule, but it is in positive violation of the law. The ministers, however, dislike very much to go without a uniform. They are conspicuous in their plain clothes, and are, in fact, the only people but the court newsman without a court dress, and they conform to the violation unscrupulously. Some years ago, one of them had a right to wear a military uniform, and he has been the envy of all his successors since.

The Queen, nevertheless, was entirely in the wrong in deciding upon the dress of a foreign envoy. She receives the Turkish Ambassador in his trousers and fez, because this is the costume in which he presents himself to his own sovereign, and she has no right to make the American Minister show his legs. If the United States Government should peremptorily forbid its representatives to appear at balls and concerts unless in the dress they wear at the levees of the President, Her Majesty would be obliged to yield. The ambassador who carried his whole retinue to court, in spite of the rules, succeeded; and whenever our ministers show similar pluck, they will win a similar victory.

It is true there seems as much reason why a uniform should be worn by officers in the diplomatic service as by those in the army and navy. All alike may be called upon to represent their country abroad. But having taken a national stand, it is not becoming to recede from it. The simplicity of the rule is not only significant of republican feeling, but in accordance with all modern tendencies. Foreigners have become familiar with the fashion, and many approve it. While Mr. Pierrepont was Minister at London he attended an opening of Parliament in plain clothes, and the London press declared that the simple dignity of his appearance contrasted favorably with the gorgeous array of barbaric envoys and European ambassadors. The Japanese and some of the South American legations have already adopted the simpler mode, and when President Grévy, of the French republic, first received the diplomatic corps they presented themselves in frock coats and trousers, out of deference to the democratic idea. On the whole, it might be well for the State Department to insist that its subordinates should obey the law.

## XIV.

### MANNERS.

THE effect of rank upon those who possess it is certainly vulgarizing. It is common, I know, to suppose and assert the contrary. The refining and exalting results of an aristocracy are always proclaimed by its advocates. We are told that a class set apart from the rest of the world and above it, is sure to be superior both in refinement of breeding and distinction of character. The great mass of English writers have constantly maintained that the upper class of their countrymen set a brilliant example to the world at large, in manners, if not always in morals; and the nobility has been viewed by most of the English and by all Americans through the atmosphere created by these writers, themselves bred to believe their aristocracy exceptionally superior and refined.

But the English men and women of letters are not members of the aristocracy. They belong emphatically to the middle class; and if some of them are now and then admitted to the houses of the great it is not as equals, but to amuse and interest the nobility. They are always at the tail of the procession to dinner, where the most liberal peer will think them in their place, an opinion in which they themselves are certain to agree. It is rarely, indeed, that they get so far as this, and only a very few of them ever see the intimate life of the aristocracy. But, being people of sentiment and imagination, and, in intellectual qualities, often far superior to the upper class, they make up their minds what the manners of a great aristocracy should be, and describe them accordingly. Even when in their own persons they have penetrated behind the veil, they are either so awe-struck at the privilege, or so prepossessed by their partialities, that their vision is blurred, and they see and tell what they think exists, not what is actually before their eyes. It is the glamour that genius has thrown around the aristocracy that gives it the brilliancy and fascination that have dazzled the world. The pictures of De Gramont, Horace Walpole, and Lord Hervey, aristocrats themselves, are very different from the flattered portraits by most of the writers of other days ; and Charles Greville's earlier volumes are proof that the most glowing descriptions of recent times are conceived in as absolute ignorance of the reality.

The high English almost always possess complete ease of manner, but almost never complete elegance, and both peculiarities are attributable to their rank. As a rule, they are remarkable for repose of bearing. There is little pushing when the aristocrats are by themselves, though plenty of it among those who wish to associate with them. The position of the nobility and their connections is so established that nobody is offended because some one of higher rank goes before him, nor elated when he himself precedes an acknowledged inferior. It is the new and uncertain people who struggle. To the aristocrats their rights are usually conceded without a contest. This naturally makes them calm, assured, serene.

But it also makes them indifferent, and sometimes insolent, toward the rest of the world. The fact that they are placed so high, so much above other people with education and taste and refinement equal and often superior to their own, creates a carelessness and superciliousness of behavior and feeling not only offensive, but almost coarse. If they are well bred, so much the better; but if not, they stand quite as secure. The pedestal is just as high, no matter what figure is placed on it. A duke may be a boor or a clown, a duchess may be illiterate or drunken or immoral—and there have been instances of all this within the last twenty years—but they are dukes and duchesses all the same. Their precedence is not disturbed, their notice is still an honor, their society is courted, their alliance is sought, if not by all, yet by so many that they never discover the deficiency. There are men of the highest rank who turn palaces into dog-kennels and consort with pugilists and yet marry into ducal families; and I have seen tipsy duchesses dance after dinner with shawls and castanets before ambassadors and Prime Ministers, when but for their rank they would not have been tolerated.

It is the consciousness of their superiority that makes them think it unnecessary to cultivate their manners or reform their morals. I once heard a countess account for the manner of one of the court ladies, which was indeed exceptionally soft and charming: "I suppose," she said, "it proceeds from her being always with a superior, always obliged to defer to another." This is the key to the feeling of the aristocracy. They have no need, they think, to defer, with equals or inferiors. They can gratify their moods or their whims, be amiable, or disagreeable, or indifferent, as they please. Toward those above them they are deferential in the extreme; servile it seems to an American, and certainly obsequious. With those whom they like they can be as affable as any people in the world, and their affability is the more agreeable because what is not common is always more highly prized. Like everybody else they can be civil enough when it is their interest to be so. But when none of these reasons exists—interest, or preference, or necessity—they are often cold, supercilious, and arrogant to a degree unknown in what is called good company elsewhere.

The brother of a duke not long ago paid his addresses to an American woman of fortune who was disinclined to listen to him. He persisted, however, till at a final refusal he got up from his knees and exclaimed: "Oh! you cannot understand us. You are not made of the same clay." Our countrywoman remembered his lordship's family history, and replied: "No, indeed. I am not descended from a king, nor his mistress."

Thackeray was once staying at a country-house where one of the high-born guests inquired after dinner: "Who is that agreeable man?" When he was told it was the famous novelist, the representative of the peerage remarked: "You surprise me. I thought he was a gentleman."

It is often not *noblesse oblige*, but *noblesse excuse*. A duchess will not return visits unless it suits her; but if she opens her house for a ball, all the world goes, and is careful to leave cards immediately afterward, so as to be invited next time.

An old peeress not now living, who had seen much of the world, said to me the night I made her acquaintance: "What do you think of us English? Are we not all very rude?" I replied that I had received too many courtesies in England to make this admission; but she went on: "Oh, I know we are ill bred. I never see a stranger but my first impulse is to be rude to him." The next day she asked me to stay a week at her country-house, and became one of my intimate friends.

I once saw a duchess drive off from a country-house where she had been visiting. Her bonnet was exceedingly shabby, and her sister, a countess, was teasing her to change it for a smarter one. "A duchess," she said, "and drive in such a bonnet!" But the duchess laughed, and replied: "Where is the use of being a duchess if I can't wear what bonnet I please?" It was all in raillery, of course, but there was a genuine feeling under the raillery.

Not long ago some one said in my hearing of the wife of an American President: "Her manners are as good as those of a duchess." "But why," it was asked, "should a duchess have better manners than any one else?" Thereupon an American exclaimed: "If they don't have good manners, what are they for?" Now, as a rule, the duchesses have the worst manners of any women in the peerage. Nobody is born a duchess, so they all must acquire their rank by marriage; and their heads are often completely turned by the elevation. Many of them have been of families quite without the pale of the peerage; they are thus absolute parvenus, and a parvenu peeress is usually downright vulgar, in her consciousness of grandeur. The daughters of dukes, who often descend in life as they go along, for the most part are better bred than their mothers.

The men, as a rule, are less insolent in bearing, if not in behavior, but just as selfish, just as determined to do as they choose, without regard to the feelings of their inferiors; and in their eyes nearly all the world are their inferiors. Their rank not only gives them this indifference; it makes them narrow, prejudiced, provincial, satisfied with themselves. With every good thing in life at their command, with everybody in England at their feet, they are naturally disinclined to effort of any sort. A duke once said to me: "I suppose I ought to go to America to improve my mind." He knew very well that his mind needed improvement, but he was a duke all the same.

There are, of course, many members of the aristocracy of admirable character and attractive qualities; some who feel the requirements and responsibilities of their position, and are worthy of their nobility. I certainly had reason to appreciate the worth and admire the charm of many individuals, but those who were charming and worthy were so, not because of their rank, but because of their personal quality. They would have been equally admirable and attractive in another rank and another sphere. Barring a certain brusqueness which almost never wears off, and the lack of that elegance which they almost never acquire, the most rounded men of the world I have ever known, not perhaps the most highly accomplished, but the healthiest in tone, the most general in information, and, when you know them well, the most genial in sentiment—those who best combine the results of life and culture—have been the very best of the English aristocracy. *O! si sic omnes!* I must say, however, that these were oftener connected with noble families than the heads of those families themselves.

But I saw also something of what is called the upper middle class—the literary and professional people. I got glimpses at the life of the great merchants and manufacturers, and I found among them quite as admirable specimens of English ladies and gentlemen as in the aristocracy; quite as genuine refinement, more regard for the feelings of others, and, unless a lord or a lady came along, quite as much innate dignity. In the presence of the aristocracy, however, they all mentally get down on their hands and knees.

The influence of rank, I repeat, is not refining. It not only magnifies the importance of externals and depreciates that of essential qualities, but it has not the effect claimed for it, of inspiring its possessors to keep themselves up to a high standard. It may do this in some rare instances, with superior natures, which would be lofty without the stimulus of rank; but with the mass of those who enjoy it, who are commonplace enough, it has the contrary effect. It encourages them to dispense with effort, it inspires an offensive pride, it relieves from the obligation of courtesy, it destroys outright that delicate consideration for the rights and especially the feelings of others, which is at the basis of every grace that makes life or character beautiful.

Talent and energy and natural moral excellence are distributed pretty equally, according to my observation, among men of every country and every grade. There are as many fools, and rakes, and knaves among the aristocracy as among the same number of men and women in any other class in England or elsewhere. There are also many vulgar people of the highest birth. There is dishonorable conduct in men of greatest rank and oldest names. The institution does not prevent these things. Blood does not tell; or if it tells, it tells the wrong way. Taking the aristocracy as a whole, judging it neither by the exceptionally excellent nor by the exceptionally vulgar or depraved, but as a class, it did not strike me as superior in ability, character, culture, or breeding to the same number of people who could be culled from the choicest circles of half a dozen different quarters of democratic America. I am sure there are 583 gentlemen in America the equals of the peers, and five or even ten thousand men and women who would not suffer by comparison with their families.

## XV.

### CASTE.

If the influence of the aristocracy is vulgarizing upon the aristocrats themselves, rendering them often arrogant, supercilious and rude, it is still more so with their inferiors, debasing the spirit and degrading the behavior to an extent incomprehensible to an American, in persons who in other respects are neither abject nor servile. When one considers the character and history of the race, the grovelling of an Englishman before a lord is one of the marvels of modern times. There is nothing like it in any civilized nation on the globe. Neither the peasant of France or Spain, nor the private soldier of Germany, nor the lazzarone of Naples, nor even the emancipated Russian serf manifests in the presence of a superior that conviction of the existence of a caste composed of his "betters," which marks the educated Briton of the middle class. The sentiment is really more remarkable in the educated than in the ignorant, for in the latter it can be excused or comprehended; but the prostration of spirit and manner, the uncovering of the whole being, without any purpose or aim of sycophancy or interest, in a man or woman of culture and refinement and character, because of the presence of a person of rank transcends explanation. The very word "betters" has a meaning that is shocking to think of.

A woman of rank once asked me what, of all I had seen in England, struck me most forcibly. I had no doubt whatever, and answered: "The distinction of classes, the existence of caste." "But," she inquired, "do you really mean to say that in America the great merchant's daughter does not look down on the little grocer's daughter?" "Perhaps," said I, "the great merchant's daughter does look down, but very certainly the little grocer's daughter does not look up;" and the whole company was horrified at the idea of a country where the little grocers' daughters "don't look up."

This, indeed, is the difference between English and American life. In England everybody looks up. The most accomplished scholars, the men of science and letters, the artists, the great lawyers and physicians, even the politicians born without the pale, all look up to the aristocracy.

Mr. Gladstone and Mr. Disraeli, undoubtedly the two greatest statesmen England has produced since the days of Fox and Pitt, who have swayed the destinies and moulded the political character of the country for nearly a quarter of a century, each sprang from the middle class, and neither ever freed himself altogether from his awe of the aristocracy. Gladstone has done more to transmute liberal ideas into realities than any other Englishman that ever lived; yet not long ago he used these words: " So far as a man in my station can be supposed to understand or enter into the feelings of one of the rank of a duke;" and Disraeli, although he made himself a peer, could not get over his admiration and reverence for a born nobleman. His own adherents made this weakness their butt. Even after he had negotiated the treaty of Berlin, had snatched Constantinople from the grasp of Russia, and received the Order of the Garter from the Queen, I heard Tory wits, both men and women, laugh at his fondness for dukes, and declare that he was never so happy as when seated between duchesses, no matter how ugly or old.

For it is not enough to belong to the nobility; you must inherit the title to feel like an aristocrat. The law lords are always slightingly spoken of as new creations; people tell you how they are descended from barbers and tailors; and any duke with proper sentiment would rather his daughter were married to a stupid country squire of ancient family than to one of your modern Lord Chancellors. It is not till the blood of two or three generations has washed away the stain of plebeian origin that they take their place without uneasiness among the peers.

It is not only the chiefs in politics who are affected by the feeling of caste. In 1874, when Mr. Gladstone withdrew for a while from public affairs, the Liberals were obliged to select another leader. Mr. Forster was then by all odds their strongest and ablest man, but they had also Sir William Harcourt, Mr. Bright, Mr. Childers, Mr. Goschen, and others distinguished for intelligence and accomplishment. Yet the Marquis of Hartington, possessed of no striking qualifications of character or capacity, only the heir to a dukedom, was preferred. Had it not been for his rank he would never have been thought of; but all, it was said, could submit to his pre-eminence without humiliation. No one could object to a leader of so exalted rank and inconspicuous intellect; while if Forster or one of the others became chief, it would be a reflection on the abilities of those who were not preferred. And this was in the Liberal party of England!

Literature hurries after politics to bend before the lords. Froude and Lecky have written with all their force and eloquence on the "Uses of the Aristocracy" and the "Landed Gentry," to which they do not belong. They are as able and accomplished as any men in England to-day, and at least the intellectual equals of any living peer; but they want some one above them—some one "to kotow to."

A literary woman, whose name and works are deservedly popular both in England and America, and who had seen enough of London society, one would suppose, to accustom her to the presence of persons of rank, could never overcome her awe for the upper classes. I went one day to call upon a friend, who told me that the novelist had just left the room, and that upon entering she had exclaimed: "Oh! I am such a snob that I am ashamed. I have been taking tea at a house where a countess came in, and it fluttered me so that I couldn't take off my gloves, and spilt all my tea."

And so, all up and down the scale. I once heard a woman of fashion say of some young girl just entering the world, who was remarkable for her self-possession: "She could go into a room full of duchesses and not be afraid."

A great merchant said to me when we were talking of the English love for sport, which in its excess I did not commend: "But how shall our aristocracy be amused? We must amuse our aristocracy." He evidently thought it one of the duties of the English nation to amuse its aristocracy.

When General Grant was in England he did not confine his visits to the nobility. He was the guest of the Mayors of all the prominent towns, and of manufacturers and merchants and other middle-class people, many of them as charming and cultivated in their way as any of the aristocracy. But they could not conceive that a mere ex-President was the equal of an earl. At one manufacturing town he stayed at a house where every honor was paid him and every courtesy extended. But his hosts took him to visit the steward of a lord who lived near by; he was permitted to see the state apartments in the absence of "his lordship," and he lunched in the land steward's room, and not in the earl's. The steward was probably an abler and better educated man than his master, and General Grant was too good a democrat not to appreciate this fact and to respect his host; but if he had been an English nobleman, neither steward nor manufacturer would have dreamed of entertaining him.

Not many years ago a statue of Mr. Peabody was erected in London, the work of our gifted countryman, Story. The Prince of Wales was present at the unveiling, and Mr. Motley, then Minister to England, delivered the address. It was an impressive circumstance—the commemoration by Englishmen of the munificence and charity of an American, who had bestowed his munificence on Englishmen. The presence of the heir to the throne and of the American Minister made the incident international; but the American artist was not invited. The city authorities of London looked upon him as a stonecutter, or at best as a tradesman who had sold them the result of his labor. Mr. Motley had to make a persistent application before they consented to include the sculptor in the ceremonies of which his own work was not only the principal ornament, but the occasion. In the eyes of the London citizen an artist is not an aristocrat; he is no better than one of themselves.

Adelaide Kemble Sartoris once told me a story about herself that illustrates the social situation in England. A great lady—which Mrs. Sartoris said she was not—had sent out cards for a ball, of course to the aristocracy. The woman of genius was about to give a dinner: her dinners were famous, for the company was of the rarest and choicest kind; poetry and wit and science and art came to her table often rather than to a lord's. The great lady wanted to go to one of these dinners, and sent word to Mrs. Sartoris that if she would ask her to the dinner, Mrs. Sartoris and her daughter might come to the ball. Mrs. Sartoris said she wanted her daughter to be seen at so grand a house, so she ate her portion of dirt and exchanged invitations with the peeress. The great lady went to the dinner, and the great genius and her daughter went to the ball.

I knew a clever American who had been struggling for a long while to get into English society, and had not succeeded. He was in every way fitted, but he had not the entrée or the introductions. At last he got afloat a little and asked me to dinner to meet some lords. The dinner was given to show his success; but the lords were all clever, and they went to his table because their host was also clever, and they knew they would enjoy themselves, not because they thought he was of their world. One of the company said to me that my countryman was getting along, but he couldn't be considered to have succeeded till he could get stupid lords.

The feeling of which I write extends to every sphere; it permeates England. The reverence that Gladstone and Disraeli showed is parodied in the sentiment of the servants, who regard the lords as beings of a different race from themselves. Even when the great people condescend, the servants never allow their own heads to be turned. When the master dances with the housemaid or the mistress with the butler, no liberties are taken in return. The great gulf is still impassable. Mr. Auberon Herbert is the brother of the Earl of Carnarvon, but a radical. He prides himself on ignoring the distinctions of rank. When he hires a new servant he is said to ask him to tea, and he offers his hand to the menials of the noblemen whom he visits. A butler, who did not refuse this honor, afterward spoke of it with sorrow and deprecation to his own master. "I know my place, my lord, and that is more than Mr. Auberon Herbert knows his."

This persistent humility is common with class, and is manifested even toward republicans. I once found it convenient to assign to my valet a room in a part of the house near my own, and thought he would be pleased with the situation; but he told me respectfully he didn't like it at all. He was a servant, not a gentleman; he didn't want to be treated like a gentleman, nor to live in a gentleman's apartments. It was not proper.

They sometimes show this same appreciation of propriety in a different way. A cook, some time ago, took service with a physician who was a baronet. She knew her master's title, and did not suspect his occupation, but as soon as she discovered the reality she gave warning. She had only been used, she said, to living with the gentry.

I recollect visiting the ruins of Raglan Castle, where the porter, in showing the great hall, is sure to announce that here once feasted a hundred and forty lords and gentlemen, every one of whom was proud and honored to serve his Grace the Duke of Beaufort. Soon afterward I was staying at the country seat of the present Earl Fortescue. Mr. Motley was also a guest, and, reviving his historical lore, he reminded his host that in other days an earl would have been served by attendants kneeling. The actual service offered to dukes by lords and gentlemen is nearly past, but the parasites of the modern peers are as obsequious at heart as their predecessors, and if the lackeys are not still on their knees at table, they are prostrate all their lives in sentiment.

I could fill pages with proof of the reverence for rank which many of the English besides Lecky and Froude defend, declaring that it exalts and refines the people who pay it: we all need something to venerate, they say. But the question is whether rank is the thing. In England, however, there is no question. The greatest nobles feel themselves honored by attendance on royalty, and their servants are conscious of no degradation in the duties they perform lower down, while the culture and genius of England are proud to pay both homage to the Queen and obeisance to the lords. To Americans this feature of caste is the most curious in the entire national character. That in the country of Carlyle and Bright, of Huxley and Mill, where the last results of modern thought and material civilization are soonest reached and often widest spread, where law and freedom are at least as universal in their prevalence as in America—this relic of barbarism should still survive, wrought into the very nature of the people—is as wonderful as if amid the congregations of Westminster Abbey or St. Paul's one should suddenly stumble on the worship of Isis or of Jove.

## XVI.

### ILLEGITIMACY.

One of his subjects said that Charles II. was the father of many of his people in a literal sense. He recruited the ranks of the nobility largely with his children and their mothers, and at least five English dukes to-day can trace their lineage to the monarch who left no legitimate descendant. One of these had a father-in-law who boasted a similar connection with a later sovereign, and of course was titled. The two noblemen were at a levee together, some years ago, and as the carriage of each stood at the door the duke said to his father-in-law: "How do you use the royal liveries?" Whereupon the other descendant of kings replied: "How do you?" One had the same right as the other.

These offshoots of royalty claim all the distinction that their birth confers. The daughter of a ducal house prides herself on her likeness to her great ancestor, Nell Gwynne, whose portrait hangs in her drawing-room, so that all who come can compare. You can pay her no higher compliment than to notice the resemblance which proves her royal origin.

The royal favors have been extended even in recent times. Charles Greville sets forth with great minuteness the relations between George IV. and the Marchioness of Conyngham. One should be well up in genealogy to go about in London society; and, though I had lived in England many years, I once came near tripping on this subject. Greville's revelations and recollections were the talk of the town, and when I went of a Sunday to call on a countess (now dead), who was fond of gossip, I asked if she had read the volumes. "Yes," she said, "but I must tell you at once, Lady Conyngham was my grandmother."

The book was very generally disapproved by the relations of those whose imperfections it exposed, the Queen among the number; for Her Majesty's uncles were the principal offenders against morality, of their time. The editor defended his disclosures by referring to the "Life of the Prince Consort," which revealed the secret and domestic history of the Queen. But the stories there told were all favorable to the royal family; Her Majesty, like the rest of the world, prefers to select for herself the point where she draws the line. It is true, she had no scandals to conceal in her own career; but I knew at least half a dozen grandchildren of William IV., none of whom were descended from Queen Adelaide. Yet they all had titles, or, as one of them said, "handles to their names." They also inherited the peculiarity to which they owed their connection with the Crown. Divorces were common in the family.

Illegitimacy, however, in England is not confined to the descendants of royalty. The nobility emulates the example set by a long line of sovereigns. In the exalted circles of the aristocracy the bastards of peers go about bearing the family names, and daughters whose mothers are unrecognized marry into families as "good" as those on the paternal side. There are even instances of sons born before the marriage of their parents, whose younger brothers inherit titles to which the elders would have succeeded, but for the neglect of their mothers to go to church in time; the legitimate and illegitimate children can claim precisely the same progenitors. Some of these premature sons are to-day ministers at foreign courts, others have been masters of ceremonies in royal houses, while dukes and earls have been able to find places for the spawn of shame in the army, the Foreign Office, and even in that Church whose rites they had themselves neglected to observe.

God knows the unfortunates are not to blame; but to make their birth a distinction and an advantage is a greater enormity than the offence to which they owe their origin. A Countess of Cardigan had once been the wife of Lord Cardigan's staff officer; but she deserted her first husband for his ef. A divorce ensued and a second marriage. A peeress not now living told me this story at her own table, and not having studied the family tree of my hostess, I innocently inquired if Lady Cardigan had been received in society. Here one of my neighbors purposely interrupted the conversation, and I perceived there was reason not to push my inquiries. After dinner I was told that the mother of my hostess had committed the fault of Lady Cardigan. The lady herself had spoken of her father, who was an earl, without a shade of reticence or embarrassment, and only some ignorant republican like me ever reminded her of the mother to whom that father was never married.

The famous Lady Waldegrave was married to two brothers in turn: first, to Mr. Waldegrave, the natural son of the Earl of the same name, and afterward to his brother, the legitimate heir, so that she was Mrs. Waldegrave and Countess Waldegrave successively. In this instance the father had preferred the child of shame, and left the bastard the bulk of his property, which was unentailed; but the fortunate lady who married first the wealthy brother and then the titled one, secured both fortune and rank without going out of the family. Her marriage with Lord Waldegrave would have been invalid, according to English law, which prohibits a marriage with a deceased husband's brother, but Mr. Waldegrave, being illegitimate, the son of nobody, was also the brother of no one, in the eye of the law. Had there been, however, a son by the second marriage, and an earldom at stake, the next heir would undoubtedly have disputed the legitimacy of the issue. But the question did not arise, and the violation of one law rendered possible the evasion of another.

Some of the aristocracy exhibit a fidelity in these irregular relations not always displayed toward more respectable partners. A nobleman who died while I was in England was devoted to a woman whom he refused to marry. He was no longer young, but when his companion fell ill he nursed her with the tenderness of the fondest husband, and when his cares proved vain and she passed from his arms—let us hope, to a better life—his grief so overwhelmed him that he could not survive the loss. In six weeks he followed her to the tomb. This touching constancy is characteristic of the family, which has shown in several instances how love can rise superior, not only to considerations of rank and station, but to morality and public sentiment. Their devotion, however, has never necessitated the sacrifice of position or precedence. During the present generation, they have filled important stations in diplomacy, secured the grants of successive peerages, and married into families even higher than their own—that is, when they married at all.

It is not to be supposed that the aristocracy are

without virtue. There are houses and circles as pure as those of the Queen; but there is hardly a family in the peerage that has not, like the Queen's, its admitted illegitimate connections. There is probably no more immorality among the upper classes of England than in the corresponding caste in other countries, or possibly than in the wealthiest and most pretentious circles in our own. But there is this difference: in America acknowledged immorality is a bar, while in England it detracts from neither rank nor station, and men and women have consideration not only in spite, but because of illegitimacy. In one country people are ennobled and received because they are bastards; in the other the shame is hidden and the stigma concealed.

An American woman, whose name is well known, was staying at Homburg with a duchess, who persisted in visiting the unmarried companion of a royal personage. The American was not sufficiently accustomed to aristocratic ways to consider the acquaintance an honor, and warned her ducal friend not to speak to that woman when they were together. Soon after this they passed the lady on the promenade, and the duchess could not bring herself to reject the recognition of a royal favorite; whereupon the American, though she had her own weakness for rank and was fully impressed by caste, indignantly left the two Europeans to their own company, and walked home alone.

The influence of rank is unfavorable to virtue, because it not only shields vice, but actually exalts immorality. A fault is more venial in a duke than in a man of lower degree. A slip in a woman of high position is easier overlooked and sooner forgotten; and there are peeresses to-day who have been divorced for cause and remarried, and who are received. This would not be if they were not members of the aristocracy. Even women who have lost their position in America, have regained it in England. One of these had a great success in the highest circles of London until finally her history became known. She then went in tears to one of the leaders of society and exclaimed: "You surely don't believe these horrible rumors about me?" To which the countess replied: "My dear, if they were all true, I shouldn't think any the less of you."

It is not true that the same thing occurs here in the same open way. Rank in England often enables its possessor to ignore or defy the shame that here would follow the sin; but the stigma blazes boldly beneath a coronet. When the late Lord Chief Justice of England could take a woman whom he had not married on judicial tours to be received by provincial dignitaries, and respond to toasts as a bachelor while his grown-up daughters sat by his side, the state of society is certainly different from that existing in America. And this difference is the direct result of aristocracy. A class is placed so high that it can make a social law for itself and defy the opinion of a world composed of inferiors. At least half a dozen peers of the realm have married women of public lives, and these women belong to the peerage. Their names must be set down in Burke.

## XVII.

### SERVANTS IN THE COUNTRY.

I once stayed at a famous castle, the master of which was very religious, and the servants came into chapel twice a day while he read family prayers. I recollect the long line of flunkeys in powder and knee-breeches prostrate around the earl as he prayed fervently that we might all be content with that state of life to which it had pleased God to call us. I had not been long in England then, and I thought that the prayer would be easier to grant in the case of the master than in that of the man. Later in my sojourn I should have known different. The lackeys are not democrats. They are of Pope's philosophy and thoroughly convinced that "whatever is, is right."

Descended often from a long line of ancestral menials, reaching back sometimes like that of their betters to the time of the Conqueror, or sprung from the class of farmers or farm laborers, once villeins or serfs on the estates of the nobility, the spirit of servility is innate and ingrained. They firmly believe that the purpose of their creation was to provide proper attendance for the aristocracy. "What would the gentry do if there were no servants?" I have more than once heard them exclaim.

Their duty in life begins early. A fortunate boy in the country is taken up to the great house as soon as he is able to trot about on errands; he carries the bag to the post, or helps in the stables, or, if especially favored, is made steward's-room boy at once, and waits on the upper servants until he is promoted to livery. He is trained in all the etiquette of the servants' hall, says "Sir" and "Ma'am," not only to those great dignitaries, the butler and housekeeper, but to the valets and ladies' maids as well; and learns to speak with bated breath in the presence of the aristocrats themselves. The girl's first function in life is to drop a courtesy when her betters pass her on the road, or to open the gate at the park lodge for the gentry to drive by.

After a while they rise, the one to the post of footman, the other to that of housemaid or kitchen maid, and so on through the degrees, till the lucky ones arrive, perhaps, at the climax of back-stairs grandeur, and are housekeepers and butlers themselves, always imbued with deference for their many and varied superiors, and always exacting the homage due themselves as they ascend.

In a great house thirty or forty indoor servants is a common number, and often there are as many more in the stables, and still as many others in the gardens, or the glass, as the conservatories are called. One nobleman that I knew was master of the hounds and kept seventy horses, and for every two horses a man. At an entertainment in the country—a sort of pageant or play—I heard some one say that a hundred of the servants came into the great hall and stood behind the guests; the remainder were on duty elsewhere. Several times, in large establishments, I asked permission to visit the offices; and the kitchens and still-rooms and sculleries, the larders and laundries, the gun-rooms and plate-rooms and brushing-rooms, the housekeeper's room, the pantries, and the servants' hall, made a labyrinth of labor difficult to explore. In making the rounds I was taken to the nurseries and the school-rooms, for tutors and governesses are only a higher sort of servant in England. They live and eat apart from the gentry, and often get less wages than valets and ladies' maids. I saw, too, the bed-rooms and the linen-rooms and the rooms where the maids were making up clothes, all rising when their mistress entered. I visited the stables and the carpenter's shop, even the butchery and the brewery—for many of the large proprietors kill their own meat and brew their own beer. Each servant is allowed beer money as well as wages, or else supplied with so many glasses, or sometimes literally horns, of beer.

Usually the servants of the aristocracy are allowed five meals a day. Their early breakfast is at seven, before the family has risen; there is lunch for them at eleven, dinner at one o'clock, tea at five, and a supper at nine. At most of these meals meats are provided, and at two or three of them beer is served. The food is well cooked and savory; they sit down to soup and pastry, to fruits and vegetables in their season; and altogether a table is spread better than many of what is called the middle class can afford. Indeed, servants in England can hardly be said to belong to the lower class—certainly not the retainers of the aristocracy. The attendance in the servants' hall is excellent, decorum is maintained, and the more punctilious perform among themselves many of the ceremonies they have watched from behind the chairs of the nobility.

They have their privileges, and stickle for them as strenuously as the lords. A butler often gets a hundred pounds a year in wages, but his vails amount to at least a hundred more. Servants have been known to stipulate, when they were hired, for plenty of entertaining, so that they could count on their perquisites. At some houses, however, the attempt has been made to break up this inhospitable tax upon guests. There are noblemen who increase the wages of their servants on condition that they accept nothing from visitors, though the same personages usually make handsome presents when they visit themselves. To people of limited means the consideration of servants' presents is a serious one, and makes visiting sometimes more expensive than staying at home. But the custom is rooted, and the perquisite will not readily be abandoned. The story is old of the gamekeeper who refused to receive a sovereign from his master's guest. He would take nothing less than paper, and the smallest bank-note in England is for five pounds.

The cooks in large establishments have for one of their perquisites what are called the drippings, the remains of uncooked meat and game. One man of large fortune told me that, wishing to distribute these fragments to his poorer tenants in the neighborhood, he offered his cook two hundred pounds a year for the privilege. But the successor of Vatel refused, and the aristocrat was helpless, unless he gave up a *chef* who had hardly an equal in England.

In the presence of their masters the English servants maintain a manner that may almost be said to be refined. It is quiet and subdued; too obsequious perhaps to suit the democratic idea, but otherwise unobjectionable. This manner, however, is something like the livery, put on for their superiors, and laid aside, I suspect, as soon as they are alone.

In many old families there still lingers among the retainers an attachment for those they serve, a fidelity and devotion that recall the feudal feeling, and which are returned by a protection and interest that make the tie a not unlovely one. I knew instances of friendship on both sides as sincere and loyal, if not as familiar, as ever exists among equals.

I was staying once with a young nobleman who had a crowd of peers for guests. We had been dining some miles away, and drove back late at night in what is called an omnibus. The valet of one of the visitors, a lad of nineteen or twenty, stood on the steps without. By a jolt of the carriage this youth was thrown off into the road, while we were still some distance from the house, and the whole party alighted to look after him. He was unable to walk or to endure the motion of the carriage, and a couple of viscounts, an officer of the army, and a baronet carried the valet a quarter of a mile up a steep hill, then bore him into the room of the master of the house, and one tore open his shirt to look for his wound. There was no surgeon, so they bathed his breast and his forehead themselves, and the youth lay on the nobleman's bed till it was certain he was not seriously injured. Not till then did the gay young rollickers assemble below for their late carouse.

I knew of another nobleman whose eldest son

was standing for Parliament. The contest was keen, and the excitement in the family extended to the servants. Finally, the heir was elected, and the news was brought to the Earl and the Countess as they stood on the steps of the house in a crowd of friends and followers. The butler, a very respectable man of fifty or more, who had been in the family all his life, was unable to contain his delight. He rushed up to his mistress, threw his arms around her and kissed her, and the salute was forgiven by the lady as well as the lord. I did not witness this demonstration of fidelity, but I was told of it by an Englishman who was present, and pronounced it unusual, but not inexcusable.

The Queen, it is well known, sets the pattern in this consideration for personal retainers. She not only visits her gillies in the Highlands, but the servants on all her estates; she attends their balls and christenings and funerals; she invites them at times to entertainments at which she is present in person, an honor she never pays the nobility; and her affection for her devoted John Brown she has been anxious to make known to the world.

Twice I was present at country-houses, when the servants joined in a dance with the family. Once it was after a servant's wedding, which was, of course, an event. On the other occasion, at a well-known lodge in the Grampians, a Highland reel was proposed, but there were not ladies enough to go round, so the best-looking of the housemaids were brought in and placed in the line with marchionesses and the daughters of earls. One was by far the prettiest of her sex in the room, and the heir of the house didn't like it at all if any of his guests danced too often with this maid. But none of these young spinsters presumed on the favor that was shown them; the distance in rank was too great to be bridged by any transient familiarity. It was the very consciousness of the gulf that made the condescension possible.

At the house of a nobleman who had a crowd of sons, and these always a crowd of boyish visitors, the whole frolicsome party was sent off nightly after the ladies had retired, to a distant tower of the castle, where they might make as much noise as they pleased. They drank, and they smoked, and they played cards, and had two or three of the footmen told off to them, who stayed up half the night with their young masters, to wait on them, and amuse them. The young men were all of the same age, and the gentlemen often invited the servants to a cigar or a glass, and not unseldom to a turn at the gloves, for most young Englishmen box. They played fair; the lords and the lackeys wrestled together on an equality. The servant might get his master down, if he could, and if the valet struck out from the shoulder, the gentleman took his punishment like a man. Only when the lords went to bed the lackeys had still an hour in the brushing-room, whitening the hunting-breeches of their masters for next day's field.

In this same family there was once an attempt at private theatricals. The play was "Box and Cox," and no one could be found for the landlady, till finally one lordling proposed his valet, a smooth-faced footman of nineteen. So William was dressed in woman's clothes and played *Mrs. Bouncer* with his master and another nobleman before all the quality. He was greatly applauded. But how it would have done to give him the part of a lord I don't know. I doubt if he could have divested himself sufficiently in that presence of his awe for his titled associates. Below stairs he might have assumed the rôle of an aristocrat and succeeded. I should like to have seen him attempt the grand air.

The servants of the great, like the aristocracy themselves, must be amused. The necessity is recognized. There are houses where they have a billiard-room and a card-room. They ride to hounds behind their masters. They boat with their betters. I have seen a valet for coxswain and earls in the crew, and one lord is well known to have borrowed from his man and never to have paid. There are often matches at cricket between the gentlemen and the servants, with the mistresses and maids looking on.

Indeed, it is said that some ladies amuse themselves with the low-born swains after a fashion not so innocent. I often heard the name of a duchess, not now living, connected with that of her groom of the chambers, and a countess who waited at Windsor was discovered caressing her footman in her own drawing-room.

It is true rich men's daughters in America have fallen in love with their coachmen. Passion laughs at the barriers of position on both sides of the sea; but here the lovers marry. In England, in most aristocratic eyes, marriage would inflict a still more indelible stain. It would affront the sentiment of caste.

## XVIII.

### SERVANTS IN TOWN.

THE servants, like the aristocracy, are seen to far less advantage in town. The entire establishment of a nobleman is seldom brought up to London, and footmen and housemaids are often hired for the season. These vicarious servitors, of course, have none of the devotion of permanent retainers, and pretend to little attachment for their masters, who hardly know them when they see them, the retinues are so enormous. I used to visit a duchess who got very indignant when only six footmen waited as she went to her carriage. "Where are all those men?" she would ask, as she looked around. "But she is justly punished for her pride," said one of the family; "since the duke died she has only four."

The footmen are usually great strapping fellows, selected for their height and the size of their calves. A tall one fetches more than a short one, and many ladies are particular that they shall be good-looking. In great establishments there is one called "her ladyship's footman," for especial attendance on his mistress, and she naturally likes him to be presentable. The advertisements in the *Times* always mention if a man is more than six feet high, for every inch is worth at least a pound a year in his wages. They make a fine sight with their breeches and their buckles; and powder refines the face, as ladies very well know. But they are an expensive luxury. There is a tax of a pound a year on every man-servant, and two pounds if he is in powder. Some of them are obliged to wear wigs, for the livery of certain noblemen requires it. I knew a family who always put their people into green wigs when they went to court; it was the hereditary color for ceremony.

State liveries, of course, are grander than those for ordinary occasions; the lackeys have their court dresses like the lords. An unaccustomed eye might easily mistake the master for the man in the crowd of gorgeous frippery and uncovered legs about the palace door. Formerly there was a certain way to tell a gentleman: he never carried a bouquet. But the test is not unfailing: flowers have nearly gone out of fashion for footmen, as well as canes. Favors, however, are still worn at weddings, so huge that if the mode were attempted here, the unfortunate wearers would be taken for lunatics. But all this paraphernalia is familiar in London. In fashionable quarters you often see footmen walking the streets in powder and without their hats, so as not to disarrange their hair; and nobody stares.

The lackeys themselves think livery no disgrace, but rather a distinction, a proof that they serve people of importance. The more conspicuous the garb, the brighter the yellow of the waistcoat or the scarlet of the cuffs, the larger the cockade or the longer the topcoat-tails, the finer a genuine flunkey feels. Besides which, they have two suits a year, and the sale of the cast-off clothes brings quite an addition to their revenues. They never condescend to take up with the garments of their predecessors, though one thrifty nobleman, who could not induce his footman to assist in his economies, is said to have had the lace ripped from the trousers and covered his own aristocratic shanks with the altered livery. But no servant who respected his class would submit to this humiliation.

Footmen are principally for ornament. Dressed finer than their masters, fed often as well—for they drink up the heel-taps at dinner, and pilfer the pâtés and jellies, no doubt, as they take them down stairs—they lead a lazy life, sitting on cushioned carriages, or lounging in front of shops and palaces, with benches placed for them on the pavements while they wait. They are always conspicuous figures on the drive or at dinner, at the opera or a ball. People in society see as much of the servants as of themselves, and the servants see all that their betters do, and mock and despise them while they bow and obey.

If a stranger to the customs and the language should suddenly be thrust into the entrance-room at a London ball, he might easily suppose that these lordly creatures, in their breeches of plush and hose of silk, with their silver buckles and powdered hair, their easy manners and constant bows, were the especial dignitaries of the occasion; while without, the throng of fifty or a hundred flunkeys bringing up carriages or waiting to be called, watching the company coming and going, handing out the ladies, and taking orders from the gentlemen, make a part of the scene as actually as the plainer dressed aristocrats whom they serve. But it is a noisy mob in the street. They lose all their elegance on the pavement—crowding, chattering, pushing, insulting the gentlemen whom they do not know and criticising the ladies they do, incessantly shouting, "Lady Somebody's carriage," "Coming up," "Setting down," "Gone for the carriage," as often in mockery as in earnest, and altogether as insolent and dangerous a rabble as can be seen anywhere in the world. A parcel of scamps in a lockup suddenly left uncontrolled could hardly be vulgarer or ruder. They seem to revenge themselves for the restraints they submit to all the rest of their lives. Here the aristocrats are at their mercy. They must have their carriages and they can't get them themselves; and the lackeys delight in annoying and disappointing and delaying them, with only half the show of serving. One can fancy what the class might be capable of in a revolution. A night scene in front of a London ball makes one think of the *poissardes* and *pétroleuses* of Paris. The contrast with the sleek sycophancy within is terrible in its suggestiveness.

After setting down their company, the carriages usually hurry off to a beer-house, where the footman may enter, but the coachman is supposed to remain on the box, and his beer and his pipe are brought out to him. But I have often seen the boxes empty in my strolls about London after midnight. Early in the evening the fine people stay only a short while at each house; there are usually four or five parties a night before the ball, and the servants have then little time for themselves. Still they often take their own friends for a drive in the ducal equipage, or hire it out for a fare, and keep their masters waiting half an hour in the hall of some great house, the footman at last excusing the delay with a lie only half believed. The carriages can be known by the arms and the liveries; and the purlieus where they are seen, the crews with which they are crowded, tell their own tale. It is not the owners who are their sole occupants.

After the company is fairly deposited at a ball, all is safe for an hour or two, and the liberty of the lackeys begins. The coachman and footman often get drunk together; quarrels and scuffles are common; the police are called in; horses are sometimes lamed and carriages smashed, but they usually contrive to be ready to take their company home, though sometimes at the risk of their lives.

These gentry, who go to four or five parties a night, are allowed to lie late in the morning. It is daylight often and often before they turn in, and half of them breakfast just in time to wait on my lady for her shopping, or her visits in the afternoon.

In town the question of perquisites comes up again; not now, it is true, from vails or visitors; only a raw American tips a footman or a butler at a dinner or a ball. But the tradesmen's bills are settled in London, and the servants have established a system of discount which contributes materially to their incomes, if it lessens those of their masters. A shilling in a pound is the ordinary toll; I had a house in London and can speak by the card. In dividing this impost the rules are rigorously observed. The valet gets his discount on the tailor's and hatter's and bootmaker's bills; the cook on the butcher's and fishmonger's and green grocer's; the butler on the wines; he, too, has the empty bottles, so that you may not economize by retaining or returning them. The coachman is entitled to the perquisite on forage, as well as on the hire of carriages and horses, and in London most people hire at least their horses, leaving their own in the country. I once bought a harness for a certain number of pounds, but my coachman went to the harness-maker and had the bill made out for guineas, so that he might secure the extra shilling in the pound. The servant who betrayed this to me was considered false to his class.

There is little use in struggling against the system. A duke with an enormous fortune attempted to stem the tide, but succumbed ignominiously. He hired a poor gentleman to supervise his bills, and paid them through him, but the servants were in league with the tradesmen, and received their perquisites all the same; while his Grace was so badly served that the peace of his life was destroyed, and he was glad to capitulate without the honors of war. As a tradesman once said to an American Minister in my hearing: "Your Excellency must expect to pay for being your Excellency."

Another perquisite is the cast-off clothes. The valets and the ladies' maids are entitled to these, and are outraged if you make any contrary disposition of them. I once gave a child about my house some old pocket-handkerchiefs, at which my valet protested; and I heard the little one retort: "You get the shirts." They often look smarter than those they serve, wearing their wardrobes sometimes on finer figures. I have heard of ladies who sold their satins to their maids, though never of a gentleman who bargained in old clothes with his man. When lovely woman really stoops to anything unworthy, she can descend to a point that leaves our sex far behind.

The servants have their clubs as well as their masters; there are two or three, I believe, for valets and butlers, besides others for those of lower degree, for the line must be drawn. The under butler, for instance, cleans the plate, and uses his thumb in the operation till it becomes unusually developed, and an under butler's thumb is often examined when he is hired; like the calf of the footman, it is valuable according to size. Now, it can hardly be expected that a person thus marked should be admitted to the society of valets and grooms of the chamber, at least, until his thumb has been reduced to genteel proportions.

But, after all, good servants take good care of good masters. Granting them what they consider their due, giving them the consideration and civil treatment which they often deserve, not interfering with their prejudices and perquisites, one can extract a deal of satisfaction from the condition of life where such servants exist. They relieve one of many of the annoyances and petty cares that take up the time of householders elsewhere. If you find honest ones—and there are many—and if you can afford a certain outlay, there is no place in the world where servants contribute so much to the comfort of existence as in England; and if you make them friends they are faithful indeed.

When I first lived in London I had a valet who watched over me with curious care. He had only served dukes and foreign ministers before me, and considered it a great feather in my cap to possess such a piece of paraphernalia as he. He supposed as an American I must be unused to the ways of the aristocracy, and he wanted to bring me on. At first he would remind me that we hadn't paid our visits since we dined at such a house, and he once ventured to remonstrate because I visited a person of the middle class. He said I had a very good connection, and it was a pity for me to visit below my station. His station in life depended upon mine, and it hurt his consequence to be the servant of a person who dined with any but the aristocracy. I once heard him say to a fellow servant that he had been in as good company as any duke or earl in England, only he stood behind the chairs. He was in his glory when I went to court, and I thought he would expire with satisfaction when I was invited to Windsor.

The servants, indeed, are all apt to magnify the consequence of their masters in order to keep up their own. I was once driving in a park where only privileged persons can pass after a certain hour. I stayed too late, and my brougham was stopped by the lodge keeper. "Who goes there?"

But I heard my coachman boldly reply, "Royals," intimating that a royal personage was within, and we drove by in state before I could rebuke his officiousness.

However, I had my drawbacks as well. I once entered a gallery in the House of Commons reserved for diplomatists and peers, where, as Secretary of Legation, I had a right to a seat. But one of the attendants saw that I had not the foreign air; I looked homespun and British, I suppose; and he knew all the nobility; so he tapped me on the shoulder, and said: "Come out of there; you are not a peer."

## XIX.

### A NOBLEMAN INDEED.

SOMETIMES Americans attribute to an aristocracy both merits and graces that are not often centred in an individual; nevertheless, there are members of the class whose nobleness is innate, and the memory of whose acquaintance it is a delight to recall. The picture of one, especially, will linger long with me.

He was both an Irish and an English peer; of illustrious lineage and almost the highest rank; middle-aged and unmarried when I first met him; of enormous fortune and, of course, with troops of friends. His manner was the perfection of simplicity; as natural as that of a peasant, as refined as that of a prince ought to be. It made me think of the exquisite clearness of water or of a diamond. There was no suggestion of manner at all. You saw straight through it to the man.

The most definite consciousness of rank I ever discovered in him was his humility that he should be an hereditary peer. He often said to me he was a sorry legislator. He believed, indeed, that the peerage was doomed, and, though he never admitted so much, I think he believed it had no right to exist, that it ought to be swept away. But he was in no haste to bring out the broom, and very well content that the institution should last his time. Still, he voted with the Liberals on nearly every occasion— that is, when he voted at all, for he was often out of England years at a time. He was a picked man of countries; had seen Japan and the United States, as well as every European court.

In his youth, he visited with his tutor one of the little German principalities, where the British envoy at once offered to present the social magnate at the petty court. The peer was willing, but he was very fond of his tutor, a man only a few years older than himself, and a person of great refinement. So the nobleman asked the minister to present his friend at the same time; but this the punctilious representative declared to be impossible; a tutor could not possibly go to court; he would not even submit so preposterous a proposition to the palace functionaries. The young aristocrat, however, refused to be presented without his friend, and, though his name had been sent in, it was withdrawn, and the British Jonathan proceeded with his David to another dukedom where the chamberlains and the diplomatists did not disturb them.

He perceived, nevertheless, the advantages of his nobility. We were together once, for a day or two, in Italy, and I recollect his telling me that he had just left the party of a kinsman, a man of enormous wealth and great position, who had twice refused a peerage; but the peer declared he had himself received far more consideration in travelling than his relation who was not noble. The title counted with the couriers and Swiss innkeepers. He chuckled a little at the sycophancy, but it was in scorn.

He had the softest, blandest manner, the gentlest smile I have ever seen in a man, combined with perfect self-possession and dignity of bearing. His courtesy was unfailing, and not confined to deportment; it was carried into deeds. He was incessantly doing something to add to the comfort or happiness of others. I can recall a score of instances in which he considered mine; and I cannot flatter myself that I was exceptional in his regard. Once he breakfasted with me to meet an American of good position, but who was often boorish in his behavior. On this occasion the republican complained of the churlishness of the English, who, he said, never invited Americans to their clubs. He had been in London for a month and met a number of prominent Englishmen, no one of whom had shown him this civility. I blushed for the taste of my compatriot, but before the party separated the Englishman inquired of me the American's address, and the same day sent him an invitation to the most exclusive club in London.

This liberal patrician was connected with half the

nobility, and at one or two houses where I was fortunate enough to be on intimate terms I sometimes met him when there were no other guests. He was then perfectly delightful. We spent hours together. He told me stories of all the great English people, initiated me into the secrets of family histories, sparing neither national foibles nor individual peculiarities; for he was not insipid; he was a shrewd observer, and not averse to satire, for all his amiability. He knew, or had known, every one worth knowing in the highest English society. He had never known any other, and, if there was a narrowness at all about him, it came from this restriction of his English field of vision. He could describe the career and the character of every Prime Minister and ambassador for the last forty years. If he spoke of any people I had not met who he thought would interest me, he would either give me letters to them or more often write direct to them and ask them to invite me. Many a tour of visits he thus arranged, passing me on from one delightful house to another.

I was always charmed to see him when I entered a strange house to dinner, or to sit near him, whether the hosts were old or new acquaintances. He looked out for my precedence; always had me put up as high as he could, and near agreeable people; asked me whom I wished to know, and presented me with the most favorable introductions, though his endorsement was itself sufficient in any circle in England.

His heart was warm as well as his urbanity delightful. When the great fire in Chicago occurred he sent me a letter enclosing his check for a hundred pounds, which he begged me to forward for the benefit of the sufferers; and shortly afterward enclosed a second check for fifty more, regretting that the Irish troubles had so reduced his income that he was unable to contribute as freely as he desired. He said he had received too many kindnesses from Americans not to wish to do something when Americans were in distress.

He had apparently no aptitude or ambition for public life, and had never been in politics. He hardly possessed first-rate ability, yet his ideas were often original, and his penetration was keen. He was well read and spoke several languages; his taste in art and his appreciation of nature were alike refined. His opportunities, of course, had been the best, and as far as storing his mind and cultivating his taste, he had made the best use of them; but he had not turned his faculties to any graver account. He was a good master, a loyal friend, a refined and amiable associate; but he made no effort to be or to do more. Perhaps he knew his own limitations, and at least he did no positive harm to any one. His life was spent in elegant ease and unobtrusive charities. Whether this was all that he should have achieved in so splendid a position his own conscience best could declare. Since he is not living, I may say that he always impressed me as feeling that he had not made sufficient use of his advantages. He seemed aware that, with such gifts of fortune and station, he ought to have accomplished something more for his country or the world. But of how few cannot this be said in any country or in any class.

When I first met this choice specimen of the manhood of any nation, aristocratic or republican, he had an income of sixty thousand pounds, and I was told by those who knew him well that his kindnesses and charities on his own estates had made him the idol of his tenants; but the crash in Irish fortunes came, and he suffered with the rest. His steward was shot, his own life was not safe on his own property, and he was an exile from the lands his fathers had held for generations. His income fell, I was told, to six or seven hundred pounds. And then his nobility became conspicuous, for it was an attribute, not an appanage. When the drapery fell off the figure was seen to advantage. He made no complaint of the injustice of treating him as if he had been a harsh landlord and cruel master; he did not intermit his efforts to do them good at whose hand he suffered. And this was not from pusillanimity. It was not weakness of opinion or consciousness of wrongdoing. His judgment was opposed to the course of the Irish party and to the policy of Mr. Gladstone at that epoch. He may have been warped by his interest or blinded by his partiality, but he took a more decided stand in politics than ever before; he went to the House of Lords to vote in accordance with his convictions and against those with whom he had formerly acted; but neither his misfortunes nor his opinions induced him to swerve in his treatment of his tenants, or affected his feeling for them. No unkind word for them escaped his lips when he discussed the situation, which for him was so calamitous. On the contrary, I heard him excuse, if not defend them. The magnanimity of this forgiveness of injuries, which he at least had not provoked, was almost Christ-like.

The moment of his disaster was most inopportune. He had married not long before a lady of lineage equal to his own, but the wealth he had offered her disappeared, and the coronet seemed a mockery without its appendages of state and fortune. One of their relatives told me they were living in lodgings in an unfashionable part of London, and kept no carriage; "and you know what that means," said the high-born dame. "A doctor or a lawyer may set up a carriage or put it down, according as he prospers for the time; but for one of us——" and she could not complete the sentence.

Her noble kinsman did not take his reverses so

to heart. He offered his paternal acres and the mansion stocked with statuary for sale, and while waiting for the result took a modest little box near London, where he was good enough to ask me to be his guest. I was charmed to go, and of all the aristocratic residences I visited in England none so impressed me with the nobility of its master. I was received with the same courtly grace as if the mansion had been a ducal one. There was no retinue of followers, no great service of plate; a single man to wait, a table ungarnished with costly wines; but no excuses were made; there was no allusion to the change of circumstances or the lack of state. The ceremony was as punctilious, the conversation as brilliant and unconstrained, the grand air as apparent as ever. I was taken in a fly to visit earls, who evidently thought no less of their peer because of the diminution of his income; and, democrat as I was, I could not but think that if birth and rank produced such results as this unconscious dignity and enchanting grace with which misfortune was— not borne, but ignored—not every consequence of aristocracy could be condemned. Only I insist that this—I wish I might call him friend—would have been just as much of a nobleman if he had been born an American and a democrat. He was one of nature's aristocrats.

## XX.

### SPIRITUAL PEERS.

THE Church in England is a branch of the aristocracy. Bishops rank with viscounts and archbishops go before dukes. The first personage in the land, after the royal family, is "his Grace, the Right Honorable and Most Reverend, the Lord Archbishop of Canterbury, by divine Providence Primate of all England and Metropolitan." The other Bishops are not by "divine Providence," only by "divine permission." Bishops, too, are only right reverend, but an archbishop is most reverend. The heirs of the fishermen of Galilee are punctilious about their distinctions and their precedence.

Nevertheless, most of the prelates are low-born. They rise sometimes by dint of subserviency, sometimes, it is true, by force of talent and learning; but, on the whole, the worldlier arts count for more than intellectual traits, and I never heard that charity, humility, long suffering, or the other Christian graces were considered at all. These are virtues which the Prime Minister leaves to be their own reward.

For it is the Prime Minister who settles the succession to the Apostles and determines on whom the Holy Spirit shall be invited to descend. He appoints every bishop and primate in the Establishment, and selects them from his own party as regularly as when he makes a judge or an ambassador. If, like Mr. Gladstone, he is a man with a religious turn of mind, he is, of course, more likely to choose from his own ecclesiastical clique; but as most Premiers are not troubled with a strong religious bias, they care little whether the bishop is high church or low. The question with them is, first, whether he will support or oppose them in ordinary politics, and, next, whether he will make trouble in Church affairs. If they have no personal favorite to place and no political debts to pay, they look for a moderate man, who will not lean too strongly to either faction, but keep peace among the brethren. A mild and amiable person, without too much zeal, who will neither entangle the Premier in polemics nor inveigle him into crusades, is the sort of man most likely to be made Archbishop of Canterbury.

There is, however, a world of manœuvring and back-stairs influence, female devices, royal intrigues, and all sorts of political and diplomatic chicanery at once set in motion whenever a bishop has been promoted to a better place or a better world. The vacant post is the object of ambition to half the important clergy in the kingdom (and their wives), and one man, as human as the rest, is to decide.

There are, of course, men of ability and learning on the episcopal bench, and there are none to-day who disgrace it by their lives; but there are many who would never have been selected by Him who appointed the Apostles, nor by laity or clergy, if these had a voice in choosing their leaders. The brightest lights in the English Church are not in the golden candlesticks. The Bishop of Exeter, like the late Bishop of Manchester, has adorned his place, though the appointment of each was bitterly opposed; the Bishop of Gloucester is learned, and the Bishop of Peterborough eloquent, but both are partisans; and Liddon, like Stanley and Milman, has remained unconsecrated, while a crowd of his inferiors received the mitre which he deserved.

The Queen, it was said, repeatedly urged the elevation of Dean Stanley to the bishops' bench, but had not sufficient influence to carry her point. The story may not be true, for Gladstone certainly was Stanley's friend, and the Dean probably preferred his independence and the life of London society, in which he was a brilliant figure, to the precedence and responsibility of episcopacy, and exile to the provinces for half of every year. More than once I heard him boast that as Dean of Westminster he was subject to no diocesan. If it had been otherwise, he might perhaps have aspired to a see, for the deans often quarrel with their bishops, especially about the control of the cathedrals. There have been fierce fights over the figures on the reredos and the ornaments in the choir.

The story was also current at one time that the canon who gave up a Princess to Lord Lorne was to be rewarded for his sacrifice with a bishopric, and many a diatribe was pointed with the taunt of so discreditable a bargain. This tale also may have been without foundation, but that the rumor should have been afloat at all shows that ecclesiastical preferment, like more mundane prizes, is believed to go by favor.

A bishop often begins his career as tutor to a lord, who in due time presents him to a benefice; or perhaps he has been master at a public school, where he made acquaintance with the parents of his aristocratic pupils. If, after a while, ambition stirs within him, he begins to write political pamphlets, or preaches political sermons, or makes himself in various ways acceptable to the dispensers of sees; and finally, when a diocese falls vacant and his patron is in power, the adroit calculator and courtier is converted into a Father in God.

Even then his struggles are not over, for there are degrees in the episcopacy. One see differeth from another see in glory—and emolument. The pay of an ordinary bishop is only $25,000, while that of the Archbishop of Canterbury is $75,000 a year. One bishopric has a seat in the House of Lords attached to it, another is without this distinction; and though every bishop is by courtesy styled My Lord, and none of them disclaim the title, only certain fortunate ones are in reality peers of the realm. Of late years, in order to restrict the number of spiritual aristocrats, only two or three of the most important prelates are allowed permanent seats in the House of Lords; all the others are obliged to take turn and turn about in being peers. This makes the lesser hierarchs strive earnestly for the prize that is set before them. They declaim eloquently in favor of the minister who can promote them; they preach and pray for him; they vote for his measures when they have the chance; they talk for him in society, and finally perhaps attain the goal of their ambition, that highest seat at feasts which their Master declared is not to be desired.

But there is a drawback to their grandeur. The glory is very much like that of the monarch and the lords, a show and a sham after all. Not only because the mitres, like the coronets and the crown, are trembling on the heads of those that wear them; not only because of the imminence of disestablishment and the certainty of approaching change; but even while it lasts the glitter is tantalizing and unreal.

The great prelate who crowns the sovereign and

performs the marriage and the burial service over the royal family, has few functions of higher importance than these. In the union of Church and State the Church is subordinate, and the lesson is constantly inculcated. If the State endows and supports the Church, it must also govern and control. Parliament determines the doctrines and regulates the rubrics of the Establishment. It settles not only what vestments shall be worn and if candles may be used, but whether there is a real presence in the Eucharist, and if baptismal regeneration shall be believed. A Parliament including Catholics and Jews and infidels legislates for the Protestant Church of England, creates and deposes its dignitaries, decides upon its rites, pronounces upon its creed; and all the consecrated Fathers in God accept its decisions and conform to its commands, rather than lose their terrestrial advantages.

When this mighty fabric of time-serving and worldliness, called an Establishment, shall have passed away; when the money-changers have been swept from the temple, and the example of the Founder of the Church is followed by the Church and in the Church; these spiritual peers who now sit beside dukes and viscounts, and, for the sake of their dignities and their incomes, submit to the yoke of politicians in things spiritual and eternal; who are told by Parliament what doctrines they shall preach to their flocks, in what belief they shall worship, with what form they shall approach the Holy Table in the most sacred right of their religion, will be pronounced the veriest Esaus that ever sold a celestial birthright for a mess of earthly pottage that the world has seen.

## XXI.

## THE POMPS AND VANITIES OF THE CHURCH.

The style of the spiritual peers is in keeping with their rank. The residence of a bishop is called a palace, his seat in the cathedral is a throne. The principal servant of Him who had not where to lay his head has three mansions at his disposal— Lambeth Palace for a town house, and Addington Park and Stone House, Thanet, when he prefers to disport himself in the country. Every bishop keeps his chaplain to read prayers for him when his lordship is disinclined to perform this duty in person. The lower clergy address the members of the hierarchy with obsequious reverence; they "My Lord" them and "Your Grace" them at every opportunity. For the prelates have a prodigious amount of spiritual patronage, livings in abundance to dispense to discreet inferiors. Though their pay has been cut down, it still equals that of any minister in the Government, to say nothing of palaces and sinecure benefices and other desirable perquisites.

Their demeanor corresponds with their condition; there are no more pompous or inflated personages in the peerage. They wear breeches and shovel hats in the street and aprons at dinner, and are as scrupulous about the shape and the cut of their clothes as any courtier or Quaker going to a meeting or a levee. They are people of high fashion, too. They like the pleasures of the world as well as its dignities. The present Archbishop of York has been caricatured in the public prints as the "Archbishop of Society," and the late Bishop of Oxford was familiarly known in aristocratic circles as "Soapy Sam." An antagonist once referred to his "saponaceous" quality in the House of Lords, and the allusion was so irreverent and felicitous that society was shocked and tickled in almost equal degree.

Bishops, as a matter of course, are conservative in politics. They must, in the nature of things, approve the union of Church and State, and detest the Radicals, who advocate disestablishment. Many of them, it is true, have been appointed as Liberals. More sees of late years have happened to be in the gift of Liberal ministers than of Conservatives, and in the lists of the House of Lords you will find the bishops all classified according to their appointment. But once in place they are like the decrepid Pope who threw away his crutches as soon as he was elected; and the stanchest advocates of privilege and caste in England are the ministers of Him who declared the least among you shall be the greatest, and that His kingdom is not of this world.

Their votes can be counted on for every hoary abuse or vested wrong. Bishops have opposed every liberal measure ever introduced into Parliament; especially every ecclesiastical reform. They resisted Catholic emancipation, the removal of the disabilities of the Jews, the extension of university privileges to dissenters, and every approach to toleration, or to placing " the sects " on an equality with that Church of which they are the nobility. They fought bitterly against the disestablishment of the Irish Church, because they saw that it presaged and prepared the way for the deposition and dethronement of their own.

Their interference in politics is sometimes very positive. Not long ago during an agricultural agitation a bishop was addressing a meeting of farmers and laborers, and significantly recommended his hearers not to duck the agitators in the nearest horse-pond; his advice was understood and appreciated. At the last elections the two primates of England, the Archbishops of Canterbury and York, united in a political manifesto, adroitly inculcating the necessity of defending and maintaining the Establishment. They appeared only to enjoin caution in the exercise of the franchise; but as the Tories proclaimed and the bishops believed that disestablishment was at issue, the unprecedented archiepiscopal fulmination was as unmistakable as the episcopal allusion to a horse-pond. Yet all these right reverend and most reverend dignitaries would have denounced any resort to the jesuitical methods of the disciples of Loyola.

Usually the highest in the hierarchy are plebeian in origin, perhaps because at the start they thought more highly of others than themselves, and so could submit more easily to slights, be more subservient to power; and, as preferment often depends upon subserviency, they have been more persistently promoted. But some are temporal peers in their own right, as well as lords spiritual, and some are the sons of peers. These are right honorable as well as right reverend. They do not lose their inherited rank because of any ecclesiastical honors they may acquire. For them the glory of the terrestrial and the glory of the celestial may be combined.

From magnates such as these to colonial bishops is a long step downward, almost as great a descent as to an American Father-in-God. The colonial bishops are, it is true, right reverend, but they do not belong to the aristocracy; they have no seats in the House of Lords, no palaces, hardly a chaplain. Nevertheless, they may wear the dress of their order, and the uninitiated often call them: "My Lord;" but they are not much invited in high society. They are Christians of the upper-middle class.

The wives, alas! of even the highest clerical potentates are not peeresses. They are in sight of the promised land, but may never enter. I have often seen them marching unwillingly at the tail of the procession to dinner, and heard them express their indignation, sometimes in hardly Christian terms, that they should be excluded from the place and precedence accorded to their husbands. Their sufferings at such times are evidently acute.

Queen Elizabeth once paid a visit to a certain Archbishop of Canterbury, who received Her Majesty in a manner becoming her station and his own. The monarch, however, disapproved the marriages of the clergy, and upon leaving Lambeth she acknowledged the hospitality of the archbishop's wife with royal arrogance: "Madam I will not call you; Miss I may not; but whatever you are, I thank you." The validity of the marriages of these ladies is no longer questioned, but their disagreeable position doubtless is a relic of the ancient uncertainty.

Nevertheless the episcopal and archiepiscopal dames make the most of the positions they occupy. Many of them have not fully renounced the pomps and vanities of the world, despite their baptismal vows; they like to throw open the episcopal saloons for balls and amateur theatricals, and Solomon in all his glory was not arrayed like some of these. Others strive by every social art to advance their own position and their husband's rank, though, as often happens in other spheres, their ambition sometimes exceeds their tact. I remember a bishop, who was universally supposed to have been egged on by his wife into utterances of a political character that damaged not only his spiritual usefulness, but his temporal prospects—they so overshot the mark. Another lady was believed to have inspired her son, who wanted the post of Chamberlain of London, a plebeian but very profitable place. The young man issued a circular setting forth his own qualifications, prominent among which he mentioned that he was the eldest son of a peer, and all society tittered at the eldest son of a peer who could never succeed his father.

The pomp and circumstance that surround the English prelates once made a profound impression on some of their Episcopal brethren from America, who looked with admiring eyes on Lambeth and the bishops' bench in the House of Peers. Satirical Englishmen used to say that the consecrated republicans were sure to simper if they were called "My Lord," and some of them got breeches and aprons to wear to dinner. They said that being in England it was proper to dress as bishops in England do. By the same rule American army officers in England should wear the British uniform. I fear the right reverend fathers were anxious for once to feel like peers.

## XXII.

### CHURCH AND STATE.

THE Church of England is the church of the upper classes. Whatever it does for the people it does as their superior. It is a part of the paternal system, and assists in governing the masses as a father governs his family. Perhaps one should rather say it is a relic of feudalism, and, like the army, is still officered exclusively by the gentry. Its advocates make their boast that the Church maintains a gentleman in every parish; and no more potent engine exists to uphold and supplement the aristocracy. The parson and the squire, like the noble and the bishop, are on the same side. The Established Church inculcates submission and deference to whatever else is established; it instructs the people to order themselves lowly and reverently toward their betters, and to do their duty in that state of life to which it has pleased God to call them.

The Church in England is "established" by law. It is founded, not on the principle of divine authority, like the Church of Rome, but on the decrees and decisions of Parliaments and courts. Its head is not the Vicar of Christ, but the Queen. It is not, like our Protestant sects of every denomination in America, a voluntary association based on the consent of those who compose its communion; it is imposed on the people of England by the aristocracy, of which it is a component part. Originally "established" by Henry VIII. because he wanted to shift his wives, it remained a monument and instrument of royal authority until the lords usurped the place of the King in the English system, and then it adapted itself to the change and became the bulwark and appurtenance of the aristocracy, which it still remains.

England is divided into 12,000 parishes, in every one of which there is a resident clergyman who receives one-tenth of the income of the land. The ancient tithe in kind is commuted, but the clergy still obtain their tenth in residence, glebe, and commuted tithe. This is in addition to the revenues of the bishops and to the expenditure for the care of the church edifices. These 12,000 clergymen constitute one-fourth of the resident landowners of the kingdom. Their incomes average more than $1,500 a year. They are landowners as absolutely as the peers; for they also are tenants for life and cannot be dispossessed short of a revolution—unless in case of crime or gross immorality. They cannot, it is true, dispose of their estates by will; but neither can one in ten of the larger landholders. From the

Archbishop of Canterbury, with his $75,000 a year, down to the humblest incumbent of a parish, they are emphatically part of the landed interest. Naturally the Church is conservative. It believes, with Rob Roy, that

> "They should take who have the power,
> And they should keep who can."

The power of appointing the clergy is itself a piece of property. It is commonly attached to the land. The incumbent of a living is usually appointed by the squire or some neighboring nobleman, in whose family the privilege descends like any other inheritance. The greatest miscreant in life or infidel in belief may appoint the clergyman, if he owns the land. If a child inherits, the guardian sometimes exercises the right; and, worse yet, the right may be sold. The succession to a wealthy piece of preferment is often disposed of years in advance. You may read in the *Times*, in this year of our Lord, advertisements of advowsons, as the right of patronage is called—the "cure of souls" for sale. Often the notice mentions that the incumbent is old, and the property is so much the more valuable, for the succession will be speedier. Then the advowson fetches a higher price. The Bishop of Peterborough has stated within the present year, that out of six thousand livings in private patronage, two thousand are frequently in the market.

The squire usually appoints his second son to the benefice. The eldest inherits the estate, and the next one takes the parish; or, if there is no second son, some other member of the family gets an inning. But large proprietors, of course, have many livings in their gift, and thus the distribution extends beyond the immediate connection. Sometimes the gentleman in every parish is the scapegrace of the family, compelled to enter the Church against his will, to earn his bread and butter in a genteel way. Many incumbents hold duplicate and sinecure benefices, and employ curates to do the work for a paltry stipend, while the real owners reap the lawful and larger income. Personal fitness has little or nothing to do with the appointment, and the choice of the souls who are to be "cured" counts for nothing at all. They have no more to say about who shall be their spiritual pastor and doctor than the sheep of any other flock in selecting their shepherd, or their shepherd's dog.

Even a Jew who owns the property may present the priest to a Christian church and the church is obliged to receive him. I knew a wealthy Jewish baronet who bought an old estate, and was not contented till he had secured the advowson, which had been sold away from the property. He chuckled over his purchase and his privilege. A Catholic, he said, could not present to a living;

the laws prohibit that outrage on the Protestant Church; but the preposterous supposition that a Jew could possess the prerogative had never been entertained.

This squire by purchase built a superb country-house overlooking his parish church, which, as often happens, stood within the park. You could see it from the windows and the porch. It stood close to the new stables. But the proprietor of the older faith was very liberal; he often invited the parson to dinner, and the dependant was proud to sit at his master's table. The reverend gentleman was a fox-hunter, a card-playing parson; one of a race not yet extinct, though the breed diminishes fast. I often saw him ride to hounds in "pink," and two or three times a week he played cards for money with his Jewish patron. He was not clever, nor learned, but by no means an uninteresting or unworthy man; simply out of his place and time; a survival; like the State Church itself, a relic of customs that are nearly past.

The squire's wife sometimes played the organ for the Christian service, and I was told presented vestments; she even restored an effigy of that Lord whom her ancestors had crucified. This truly Catholic couple had crowds of Christian guests, who went to church in the park, and on Trinity Sunday prayed in the squire's own pew for "Jews, Turks, and other infidels."

The baronet and his wife were liberal in temporal things, as well as spiritual. One day the children of the village had a tea in the servants' hall, and I was permitted to attend the feast, for I was known to be curious about English customs. The mistress was present, and at a signal from the housekeeper one of the little ones said grace over the tea, ending the petition with "for Jesus' sake," and all the children bowed the head, at that name, in the Israelitish presence.

I visited another house where the master was a Protestant earl, and he, too, had his religious chuckle, though for a different cause. He was the neighbor of a family far older than his own, though not ennobled. On the ancient estate there stood a church, built long before the Reformation. The house of the squire was so near that it had once been connected with the choir; in fact, all had been one building. The bones of the family had been buried within the venerable walls, and, despite the Reformation, you may still read "Ora pro nobis" on the brasses of the pavement; but the Protestant service is said over them now. The family, however, remained Catholic, and the presentation to the church that stands under the window of the son of its founder is in the gift of the Protestant earl six miles away.

The Catholics have had their day. When the Marquis of Ripon became a Catholic some years ago, he gave up the numerous livings in his gift, and his wife or his son has the presentation now, for a woman may present to a living, though she may not sit in Parliament, nor, except in rare instances, inherit a peerage. The Catholic Dukes of Norfolk are the premier nobles of England, and have a chapel at Arundel, where they are buried in the church erected by their ancestors, but the mass must be said on the outside.

Nevertheless the chancel wall is broken down for them. They are dukes if they are Catholics, and in England the privileges of the great extend within the House of God. Armorial bearings on the walls remind the spectator of the former importance of those who rot beneath, and the pews are sometimes canopied, so that royal and noble sinners can pray with dignity.

The pews in the parish churches are often peculiar. I once stayed at a house where you stepped out of a corridor into a large, square room, carpeted, with chairs and a table, and in cold weather there was fire in a grate. One side of this pew overlooked the chancel, so that the family could sit out of sight of the congregation and participate in the service, or not, as they pleased. If the preacher was prosy they left without being observed. In great things and small the Church of England consults the convenience and the consequence of those by whom and for whom the existence of the Establishment is maintained. The church and the mansion, the palace and the cathedral, like the Church and the aristocracy, are part of one fabric, built into each other, so that one portion can hardly be removed without the whole edifice tumbling.

## XXIII.

### THE HOUSE OF COMMONS.

The influence of the Peers is not confined to their own chamber. It is through the House of Commons that the aristocracy has long exercised a great portion of its sway.

In the early part of the present century the lower House was at once dependent and corrupt. Nearly all its members were the direct nominees of the Lords, or were returned through their interest. For a member of Parliament may be returned without an election. He is nominated with the proper forms, and if there is no opposition, he is declared returned without any voting whatever. Thus 70 members were returned by 35 places in England and Wales in which there were scarcely any electors at all; 90 members were returned by 46 places with less than 40 electors each, and 37 members by 19 places having not more than 100 electors. In Scotland, in 1823, when the population was 2,000,000, the total number of persons enjoying the franchise was less than 3,000. In 1831 the county of Argyll, with a population of 100,000, contained only 115 persons entitled to vote. Caithness, with 30,000 inhabitants, had 11 voters. Edinburgh and Glasgow had each a constituency of 33 persons.

In the county of Bute, which had 14,000 inhabitants, there was only one resident elector. This voter was once the only person present at an election besides the sheriff and the returning officer. He took the chair, constituted the meeting, called over the roll, and answered to his own name. He then moved and seconded his own nomination, put the question to vote, and was unanimously returned.

In 1816, in England and Wales, 218 members of the House of Commons were returned by the influence or nomination of 87 peers, 137 were returned by 90 commoners, and 16 by the Government, making 371 nominee members. Of the 45 members for Scotland, 31 were returned by 21 peers and the remainder by 14 commoners. Of the 100 Irish members, 51 were returned by 36 peers and 20 by 19 commoners. Out of the 658 members of the House of Commons, 487 were returned by nomination, and 171 only were representatives of independent constituencies.

Seats were thus held in both Houses by hereditary right, and the control of the Peers over the constitution and proceedings of the Commons was direct and flagrant. The Duke of Norfolk was represented by 11 members, the Earl of Lonsdale by 9, the Earl of Darlington by 7, the Duke of Rutland, the Marquis of Buckingham, and Lord Carrington each by 6; and the right of the patron to control the votes and the political conduct of his members was unquestioned.

It was natural that under such circumstances seats should be sold as openly as estates. Nine thousand pounds were paid for the representation of one borough to its owner, and from £2,500 to £5,000 was an ordinary price. From the King down, all were engaged in the shameless traffic. The sale of seats was first restricted in 1809, but it continued by private arrangement until 1832, under the auspices of the Secretary of the Treasury himself.

The aristocracy that created and enforced this system is the same that exists to-day; shorn of its authority, it is true, curtailed of its proportions, but unchanged in its instincts and aspirations, hankering after its former prerogatives, fighting for every privilege, clutching after every fading relic of power.

The various reform bills have lessened, but not abolished, the influence of the Lords over the House of Commons. The control of the popular assembly may be slipping from their grasp, but they have not yet let go their hold. As late as 1838 all but proprietors in land were excluded from seats in the lower chamber, and not until 1858 was every property qualification abandoned. There is still no salary allowed to members, a provision intended to restrict admission to the wealthier sort. Even since the extension of the franchise, the members elected from the working class can be counted on the fingers. Sixty of the "representatives of the people" in the last Parliament were sons of peers, more than half were of the aristocratic caste, and one-fourth were titled. The "popular assembly" still remains in part one of the possessions and appurtenances of the aristocracy.

There are few noblemen to-day who are unable to secure the return of their eldest sons to the House of Commons. By many constituencies the heir is still elected as a matter of course. Sometimes two great families contest the seat for a county between them, as in Yorkshire, where the houses of Harewood and Fitzwilliam, within the memory of men now living, expended a hundred thousand pounds apiece in a struggle in which the eldest son of each was standing for Parliament. The Fitzwilliams succeeded, and, until 1870, no member of either family visited the other. It was my fortune to be present when, after all these years, a reconciliation was effected, and the Harewoods came to a dinner with the Fitzwilliams.

The political influence of the Duke of Buccleugh was so great that in 1880 Mr. Gladstone thought fit to attack it in the Duke's own county, where the eldest son, the Marquis of Dalkeith, had always, as a matter of course, been returned. Here Mr. Gladstone proposed himself as a competitor. It was bearding the Douglas in his hall. The struggle was fierce, and few more significant signs of the times have lately been observed than this presentation of himself by a Liberal leader in the stronghold of a Tory family. That he should have succeeded was more portentous still.

These eldest sons of peers and their younger brothers and cousins, of course, turn popular representation into a mockery. They can have no sympathies with a people rousing itself from the enthralment of centuries, while the other nominees of lords must serve their masters in order to retain their places. Mr. Disraeli entered Parliament as a Radical, but soon found it more profitable to play the part of a Tory. The Marquis of Salisbury, the late Prime Minister, the most arrant aristocrat and violent partisan of his order in the kingdom, the bitterest English enemy of democracy alive, was for years a member of the so-called popular chamber, a "representative of the people!" and he has hosts of followers there to-day, sons of peers, heirs to dukedoms—even peers of Ireland—all "commoners," supposed to balance the influence of the lords.

I have already told that when even the Liberals in Parliament were in want of a leader, they turned, not to a manufacturer, like Bright or Forster, a man of the people, but to the eldest son of a duke—the

Marquis of Hartington. But the aristocrats call themselves Liberals, the political descendants of the Whigs, cannot, in the nature of things, be very earnest for reform. Some are simply designing men who strive to lead the party which they fear openly to oppose, and hope to stem the tide by seeming to swim with the current. Others, like the Girondins of France in the first Revolution, undoubtedly believe that moderate reform is advisable, or at least inevitable, and are willing to contribute to bring it about, thinking amelioration better than demolition, and alteration preferable to extirpation. But irreconcilable differences between the Liberals and the Radicals are constantly becoming apparent. Great peers, whose families have been Whig since the days of William and Mary, are found of late on the Conservative side. The Earls of Fortescue and Fitzwilliam have gone clean over. The Duke of Argyll is on the road, while men ennobled by the present Prime Minister deserted him as soon as they were seated in the House of Lords.

A few sons of peers are liberal at heart, in spite of their position and surroundings, and if they had been born in different spheres, might have held different politics. Many years ago I talked with one of these who was then the heir of a Tory minister. I had lately arrived from America, where I had been so placed as to see from the inside all the wild scramble for office that occurs when a new

President comes into power. I made some comment on this strife, comparing it with the condition of things in England. But the aristocrat replied: "All this is sure eventually to happen here. Whatever you are we shall be." He did not seem to say it regretfully, and went on to speak of the way in which a man is fettered by circumstances. One cannot always be himself, he said, nor act for himself. Friends and position control him, and whether he will or no, he is swept on by the current in which he was born. I often thought of this conversation afterward, when the commoner had become a peer and a member of a Tory cabinet more retroactive in its policy than any in which his father ever sat, and defended measures as different as possible from any ever suggested in America.

The younger sons sometimes emancipate themselves more completely. It is more natural that they should be liberal; interest and anticipation do not trammel them so closely. There are brothers of earls who are almost radical, especially when the incumbents have many sons. But I can remember only one heir to a peerage whose love for the people overcame the instincts of his order, and he died before his fidelity could be tested by possession.

Thus the House of Commons remains to a great extent under aristocratic influences. It is impossible that the sons and heirs of high noblemen and great landed proprietors should earnestly support measures looking to the overthrow of their class, the abolition of their privileges, and the eventual dissipation or confiscation of their estates. These will always be found openly or covertly working in favor of the nobility, whose interests are now invariably opposed to those of the masses; while in any great political emergency the influence of the peers is brought to bear with prodigious force on the plebeian members of the House of Commons. The most potent engine then is always the social one. Invitations to great houses are lavished upon irresolute adversaries; peeresses leave cards on the wives of timid or aspiring members, and fashion opens its most exclusive doors to those whose votes are still, as in other days, for sale. There have been instances of men who held out long against every temptation of place or power, but finally succumbed to the blandishments of Tory duchesses. Society is conservative in London, and the path to Hatfield House, like the floor of another place not so desirable to visit, is paved with Liberal intentions and Radical promises.

Mr. Gladstone once declared that the love of an Englishman for freedom is hardly stronger than his love for aristocracy, and Sir William Molesworth, one of the most astute of recent political philosophers, asserts that this feeling in England has the force of a religion. But the god is a fetich.

## XXIV.

### THE LAND.

The landed property of England covers 72,000,000 acres. It is worth ten thousand millions of dollars, and yields an annual rent, independent of mines, of three hundred and thirty millions. One-fourth of this territory, exclusive of that held by the owners of less than an acre, is in the hands of 1,200 proprietors, and a second fourth is owned by 6,200 others; so that half of the entire country is held by 7,400 individuals. The population is 34,000,000. The peers, not six hundred in number, own more than one-fifth of the kingdom; they possess 14,000,000 acres of land, worth two thousand millions of dollars, with an annual rental of $66,000,000.

Next to Belgium, England is the most thickly populated country in the world, but the Duke of Devonshire has one estate of 83,000 acres and another of 11,000; the Duke of Bedford one of 33,000; the Duke of Portland owns 53,000 acres, the Duke of Northumberland 181,000, and in every county there are properties ranging from 10,000 to 30,000 acres in the possession of the lords. Seven persons own one-seventh of Buckinghamshire, which has a population of 175,000 and an acreage of 450,000. Cambridge has a population of 149,000, and five persons own one-ninth of the land and receive one-thirteenth of the rental. In Cheshire the population is 561,000, and sixteen persons own two-sevenths of the land, which is 602,000 acres in extent.

In Ireland the situation is similar. In the province of Munster eleven persons own one-eleventh of the land. In Ulster, a noble marquis, the grandson of George IV.'s mistress, owns 122,300 acres; the natural son of another marquis, who was probably the worst Englishman that ever lived, owns 58,000, and still another marquis, married to a woman of the town now living, owns 34,000. In Connaught two persons own 274,000 acres, and besides these Viscount Dillon holds 83,000 and the Earl of Lucan 60,000. Lord Fitzwilliam has an estate of 89,000 acres, the Duke of Leinster one of 67,000, Lord Kenmare one of 91,000 and another of 22,000, Lord Bantry one of 69,000, Lord Landsdowne one of 91,000, another of 13,000, and another of 9,000; Lord Downshire one of 26,000, one of 15,000, and another of 64,000; Lord Leitrim three of 54,000, 22,000, and 18,000 respectively. The Duke of Devonshire, in addition to his enormous English properties, has one Irish estate of 32,000 acres and another of 27,000. His eldest son is the Marquis of Hartington, recently the leader of the Liberal party in England, but his lordship was unable to follow Mr. Gladstone in his endeavors to bring peace and prosperity to Ireland. Like the young man in Scripture, he went away sorrowing, "for he had great possessions."

Scotland, however, is the paradise of the peers. The county of Sutherland contains 1,299,253 acres, of which the Duke of Sutherland owns 1,176,343. The population of the county is 24,317 souls. Six other potentates hold over 100,000 acres among them, leaving exactly 5,295 acres for the remaining 24,310 inhabitants. There, are, however, only 85 of these with more than an acre apiece.

Among the other great proprietors in Scotland are the Duchess of Sutherland, who owns an estate of 149,000 acres in her own right, and the Earl of Fife, who has one of 140,000, another of 72,000, and another of 40,000. The Duke of Richmond has one of 155,000 and another of 69,000; the Earl of Seafield (the head of the Grants), one of 96,000, one of 48,000, and one of 16,000; the Earl of Breadalbane owns 193,000 and 179,000 acres; the Duke of Hamilton, 102,000 and 45,000; the Duke of Buccleugh, 253,000, 104,000, and 60,000. The Duke of Argyll is comparatively poor; he owns only 168,000 acres, while the Queen's estate of Balmoral is a modest little property of 25,000 acres. In Inverness-shire twenty men own 2,000,000 acres among them, and in Aberdeenshire twenty-three "lords and gentlemen" own more than half the county, though the population is 244,000. The greater part of all this territory is devoted to the sports of the aristocracy, for whom Scotland is only one great playground.

Three-fourths of these noble landlords inherit their estates either from grasping robbers of the Norman type or Cromwellian conquest, or from women who sold their beauty and their virtue to kings or panders, or from politicians of the stamp of Aaron Burr or Alderman Jaehne. Walpole and Pitt were the most lavish distributors of coronets England ever had, and one of these notoriously bought with money and titles the very Irish Union which is certain soon to be dissolved, while the other was the author of the famous maxim in English politics, "Every man has his price."

The great landowners themselves seldom cultivate more than a little piece of soil, sufficient for the requirements of a single establishment. The arable and pasture land of the kingdom is let out to 1,160,000 tenant farmers, 70 per cent. of whom hold less than 50 acres each, 12 per cent. between 50 and 100 acres, and only 18 per cent. more than 100 acres apiece. In all the kingdom only 600 farms exceed 1,000 acres in extent. Many of the farmers are little better off than their own laborers, but in the aggregate they employ a capital of $2,000,000,000. With the laborers they constitute one-tenth of the working population of the country.

The laborers have no capital but the furniture of their dwellings, unless the strength of their bodies and the hard experience of toil may be considered capital. Their wages are insufficient to maintain them, and the consequence is there are a million of paupers to be supported by the State. They have, of course, no independence, and are in reality serfs of the soil. They rarely leave the parish in which they were born; until recently, if they did so they forfeited the right to relief when destitute, or to the almshouse, which every peasant looks to as the end of his laborious life. They never save; they have insufficient food; in many parts of the country their stature is dwarfish, their gait slow and sluggish, like their minds. They have no education; their only pleasure is drink. Above all, they have no possibility of bettering themselves. But it is upon their poverty, degradation, and misery that the grandeur and luxury of the aristocracy are founded. One is the direct cause of the other.

In 1880 the average wages of the agricultural laborer, the man who worked the two thousand million acres of land and produced the three hundred and thirty millions of revenue, was fourteen English shillings a week, or about fifty cents a day. Out of this he had to pay his rent to the earl or the duke, which was two English shillings, or fifty cents, a week. Bread was three cents a pound, meat eighteen cents, and butter one shilling and eight pence, about forty cents. So his fifty cents a day would not buy many pounds of meat or butter, if the family was large. For there were shoes to be got for all, clothes, fuel, lights, as well as food, all out of fourteen shillings a week, and in sight of the castle of my lord, who was rich solely because the hind was poor.

The ordinary cottage of the English laborer has but two rooms, and when the married man has a family of nearly or quite grown sons and daughters they often all sleep in one room, and not unfrequently in the same bed. The great majority of cottages are wretchedly built, often on very unhealthy sites, miserably small, very low, badly drained, and they scarcely ever have a cellar or a space under the roof above the room on the lower floor. They are fit abodes for a peasantry pauperized and demoralized by the utter helplessness of their condition.

The first summer that I spent in England I visited two splendid mansions in the south whose owners were earls. One of these showed me a hall in his castle that was restored in the time of Henry V., and the other was of the family of that Count Robert of Paris who sat for an hour on the throne of Constantinople. Both of these nobles were personally estimable, and even religious men, who undoubtedly supposed they were doing their duty in that state of life to which it had pleased God to call them. I knew of exalted and beautiful traits in the character of each that would extort the admiration of honorable men everywhere.

While I was visiting them, I attended the meetings of the British Association for the Advancement of Science, held in a neighboring town. Large parties went in each day from the palatial and luxurious abodes of the nobility, to be present at the sessions, at which an earl presided; and nearly a score of high-placed proprietors attended what interested me most of all, the sittings of the Department of Political and Social Economy. The magnates were engaged for several days discussing the condition of the English poor. I heard viscounts and baronets and bishops and earls lamenting the misery and depravity, the poverty and low wages of the wretches who lived on their estates. I heard them admit that in their part of the country a shilling a day was often the wages of a strong, healthy man, who had a wife and six or seven children to support, out of which, I heard them say, at least a shilling a week was deducted for rent. I heard that whole families occupied a single bedroom. I heard of the ignorance and stolidity, often the brutality, of the English peasants, of whom there are several millions.

Not all are in this extreme condition, but all are degraded and demoralized; and I have heard English noblemen declare that, as a class, they are more brutish—that was the word—than any other peasantry in the world. The worst things I have told are neither exceptional nor rare. I went back to the stately halls, where forty or fifty guests were feasted each night off of silver, and where the very servants were ten times better fed and clad and housed than the best off of the lower class outside; where the poor crowded around the charitable kitchen gate, literally glad to feed on the crumbs that fell from the rich man's table; and I wondered what would be the end—and how long it would be deferred—of the aristocracy of England.

## XXV.

### ENTAIL.

The land of England does not belong to the landlords. An enormous proportion of it is entailed, and the so-called proprietors are in reality only tenants for life, without the power of selling, or of determining who their successors or heirs shall be. Many estates are also burdened with settlements, jointures to widows, or sometimes provisions for younger children; or mortgaged for the debts of long-deceased owners. I recollect an earl who had to pay out of his nominal income the jointures of three countesses, the widows of his predecessors. The reigning countess told me she could not afford a house in London till the last of these ladies died; but they were long-lived, and kept up their establishments near Grosvenor Square while she was forced to remain in the country, or live for only a month or two of the season at an hotel in town.

I knew another nobleman, whose father and uncle had so encumbered a splendid property that proceedings were taken to satisfy the creditors. It was impossible to sell, or to disturb the rights of the heir; so the estates were placed in the hands of trustees, who managed them for the benefit of all concerned. A certain allowance was made to the nominal possessor and his eldest son, who made out the best they could with their stipend; but on the death of the earl the new man came unencumbered into possession of 90,000 pounds a year, with no obligation to pay the debts of his father. As the creditors were aware of this contingency when they advanced the money, they only suffered a loss the possibility of which they had voluntarily incurred.

Entail is a deliberate invention of the aristocracy to preserve the land in the hands of the few, at the expense not only of the other members of great families, but of the community at large and its individual members. If it is impossible to sell, it is, of course, impossible to buy, and rich men desirous of becoming "landed gentry" have often been for years unable to enter the territorial aristocracy. The importance of those who are called "the great" in England depends in a large degree on the possession of land. The wealthiest tradesmen, merchants, bankers, brewers, find their consequence incomplete until they can purchase estates and rank with the county families. To keep these new people out is one of the objects of the system of entail.

Nevertheless, of late years, they contrive to find

their way within the exalted company; and then immediately proceed to entail their newly acquired possessions. I knew a rich Jewish gentleman, the son of a banker, whose father left half a million pounds to be invested in the purchase of an estate, and half a million more to build a house. The son complied religiously with his father's injunction, and bought a property that had been in a single family seven hundred years; he put one of the costliest mansions in England on the site of the Crusader's manor-house; and the entail of these modern Jewish gentry was so strict that napkins and towels had to be replaced, whenever worn out, by the tenant for life, that the establishment might descend to the successor in undiminished splendor. But the son died childless, and the estate went to his nephew, who had seven daughters and no male heir. The line so carefully provided for is likely to become extinct, and the property scattered among females who will carry it into other families.

Half a million pounds, however, were left to a married sister, who herself instantly "made an eldest son," as the English say; that is, she entailed the bulk of her fortune on one child, although she had four. But the irony of fate pursued the family, and this eldest son died unmarried before his mother. A younger and delicate boy is the only male representative in the coming generation, and he cannot succeed to the name, being in the female line.

In spite of patrician precautions, the vicissitudes of fortune continue. I was once taken to a stately mansion in Cheshire, whose ancient timbers proclaimed the gentility of the master, for they had been laid in the times of the Henrys. The story that was told me in this venerable structure was piteous to aristocratic ears; but let democrats determine. The present proprietor had no sons by his first wife, and at her death he settled the property absolutely on two infant daughters, intending solemnly never to marry again. But, alas for human constancy! long before the daughters were grown he had another wife and a son. But the entail was irrevocable. One daughter was dead and the sister inherited all, and the anomaly, hateful in English eyes, is presented, of a son bearing an ancient and honorable name—but penniless, while his sister inherits the family seat, the heirlooms, and the jewels. The son absolutely goes out into the world like an adventurer to earn his bread; and all good aristocrats lament the hardship which gives to a daughter the property that in every other case would descend to the son, and leaves to him that poverty which, according to English rule, should be reserved for daughters alone.

The famous Holland House was entailed as long as possible, but at last there was no one to entail it to. The last Lord Holland left no son, nor legitimate daughter, not even a collateral heir to his title or estates, and the grand old mansion where Addison wrote and Charles James Fox was a brother's guest, where the symposia were held that Macaulay described, and where, even in the present decade, the royalty and aristocracy of England are annually received at the most brilliant out-door parties of the century—Holland House is the absolute property of Lady Holland, herself no born owner of the name, no daughter of the family, but a stranger whose title comes by marriage. This peeress is poor for a noblewoman, and has bargained with a distant and wealthy connection of the family, the Earl of Ilchester, a Fox-Strangways by name—to leave him Holland House in her will, on condition that he pays her during her life £7,000 a year. By this ignoble huckstering in an illustrious family, the time-honored structure is still preserved to the blood and name of those who made it historical—a shabby substitute for entail.

The entail and the settlements reduce the nominal income of a tenant for life, sometimes by half. They affect not only his power of disposing of the property, but his ability to improve it; for this tying up of land often prevents the so-called owner from raising money to drain, or plant, or build. There are proprietors who cannot cut down a tree without the consent of the heir. Many are entirely unable to develop the resources of their land, to improve the cottages of their peasants, to stock the farms for the tenantry—solely because of the entail. Thousands of landlords would be enriched to-day if their estates could be broken up and sold. Their debts could be paid, the property vastly improved, the whole country benefited; but all this is prohibited in order to continue the existence of a privileged class who cannot, if they would, get rid of their property, even to increase their fortunes. Entail is the incubus that rests on all—owner, farmer, and laborer.

The importance of keeping consequence and power in the hands of a few, is so much considered that even if an estate is not entailed by will or settlement, the law steps in to enforce the sacred principle of primogeniture, and whenever a man dies without a will the eldest son inherits all the land. More even than this: in order to limit the ownership of the soil every impediment is placed by the State in the way of transfer. The formalities on the sale of land are numerous and intricate and obligatory, and purposely contrived to complicate and obstruct a change of owners. The legal fees are enormous, and one of the most difficult things to do in all England is to purchase landed property. The consequence is that even if poor people accumulate enough for the purchase money, they are frightened from the attempt by the charges and difficulties; and the possession of land becomes one of the greatest of luxuries. Then too the income is small; two per cent. is a high rate of interest on land, and only the rich can afford to invest their money in this way.

The tendency, therefore, is steadily to the disappearance of small estates and the accretion of larger ones. The poor man's acre is swallowed up in his rich neighbor's domain. The class of yeomen, or small farmers owning their own properties, has almost vanished. The tenant farmers have replaced them, holding their acres by a yearly lease dependent on the good will of the master for a renewal. This is the tenure of a large proportion of the farm land of England to-day.

And this system is not only the result of circumstances, the consequence of past events now uncontrollable or irreversible; it is the object and aim of present legislation and politics. Some years ago the condition of the landlords in consequence of entail was so disastrous, that the State was compelled to intervene, but instead of breaking up the entail or facilitating in any way a change of ownership or the sale of land, the expedient resorted to was of quite another sort. The Government lent to the landlords, making the debt a charge on the land. A Parliament, composed to a large extent of landlords, voted to lend themselves money at easy rates in order to improve their lands, but refused to do anything to render the sale easy, or in most cases possible.

The State—or the class that has hitherto controlled the State—is determined to maintain the aristocracy; and nothing renders the aristocracy so secure as the system of entail. Abolish this, and the whole edifice tumbles. It is the underpinning and the foundation stone.

## XXVI.

## SPORT.

ONE-THIRD of the soil of England is devoted to the pleasures of the aristocracy, the principal of which is sport. The story is old of the foreigner who stayed at a country-house where every morning the men of the party exclaimed: "'Tis a fine day! Let's go out and kill something." The picture is not exaggerated. Many Englishmen of fortune seem to suppose they are sent into this world to hunt foxes and shoot grouse and deer. This is the object of their existence and the occupation of their lives. Among the aristocracy the man who does not shoot is an anomaly, almost a monstrosity. There must be something wrong about him.

All the arrangements of the upper classes—political or social, in town or country—are made with reference to sport. The fashionable season and the parliamentary season are determined by the game laws; country-house parties in winter and tours to the Continent in summer depend upon what are called "close times." Courtships are carried on, marriages are postponed, to suit the convenience of sportsmen. Great political revolutions are precipitated or deferred, questions of peace or war are taken up or let alone because ministers want to go to Scotland, because grouse-shooting begins in August, and fox-hunting is not over till February. The gravest crises in the history of a government are neglected when legislators are anxious to be off to the moors, and the sessions of Parliament cannot be held till the frost is out of the ground and the foxes begin to breed.

Estates are purchased and houses built because of the proximity of the covers; properties are valuable or insignificant according to the amount of game. Scores of fortunes are lost through the excessive love of sport. Every circumstance and event of English high-life revolves around this pivot, and the results are as visible as those of religion. Sport enters into politics, it colors literature, it controls society. It affects dress, manners, etiquettes, and entertainments, the relations of master and servant, man and wife, father and son; the characteristics of whole classes in the State. It is one of the principal causes and results of aristocracy to-day.

On the 12th of August the sportsman's year begins. Grouse-shooting dissolves Parliament, and all who have moors, or invitations to them, make haste to the north. There is some good shooting in the south, but the best grouse-moors are in the opposite direction. Parties of twelve or twenty are common, but the genuine sportsmen often go off in smaller numbers. In Scotland there are hundreds of small shootings let for the season at prices varying from forty pounds to four thousand, according to the extent and quality of the game; but the great proprietors of course reserve the best for themselves. On many estates there are small shooting-boxes, or still simpler cabins called shielings, plainly furnished, where half a dozen men can go without ladies, and devote a few days or weeks to their favorite pastime.

More often, however, society is combined with sport. At a great house the party is usually large. The men sally out each morning "to kill something," and sometimes the ladies accompany them. Of late years a few of these are shooters themselves. This is, of course, when the game is driven to the guns; at such times the bags made are enormous, hundreds of birds often falling to a single sportsman. The labor is less, and the glory, but the boasting is prodigious.

The shooters go out soon after breakfast—by ten o'clock always, and earlier when they are very much in earnest. The dresses are rough, necessarily; the boots heavy-soled, for tramping over the moors; the knickerbockers coarse, and in Scotland many wear the kilt. Lunch is taken on the moors, and by two o'clock it is very acceptable. Sometimes a cart comes out from the house with a hot lunch, and the ladies accompany it on ponies or in little carriages; but if the game is far from the road the gillies carry cold meat and claret in hampers. Whiskey each man takes for himself. The gamekeepers and gillies and beaters make quite a procession, with the extra guns and the game-bags. They load for the gentry, and sometimes bring in the birds, and beat, and drive, and take as keen an interest in the sport as their masters, or the dogs, which also form an important part of the company. The fresh air, the mountain mist, the purple heather, the glimpses of scenery, the exhilaration of the exercise, all make the pastime more than fascinating, even for those who have less than an Englishman's passion for "killing things."

In Scotland deer-stalking is another favorite form of the amusement. It is much more laborious, the sportsmen must walk farther, must lie on the hillside often for hours, must watch more warily, and shoot perhaps more skilfully, but the glory of bringing home a stag is great enough to compensate. The deer-forests, as they are called, contain no trees; they are simply great stretches of broken land, probably once wooded, but now bare and bleak for miles and miles; with little lochs scattered among the hills, their sloping banks covered with masses of bracken, the haunt and the browse of the red deer. These vast expanses devoted to stalking make up a large part of the estates of the Scotch nobility. Hundreds of thousands of acres are included in the deer-forests of some half a dozen dukes and earls.

A party of stalkers returning over the hills after a long day's sport, and standing out against the red evening sky, makes a picture that the stranger is sure to remember. Most of them are in Highland dress, with plaids and sporrans, feathers in their bonnets and daggers in their hose; their legs are bare, and their guns are at their shoulders. The stag is slung over a pony in the middle of the group, his antlers attesting his age. They shout and wave their bonnets and plaids as they approach, and those who have remained at home are sure to go out to meet them at the gate, to listen to the story of the day's exploits, to count the branches on the antlers, and accompany the party to the larder or the butchery, where the stag is weighed and divided. At night the man who has shot a stag is entitled to wear a red waistcoat at dinner.

A bath and a cup of tea refresh the jaded sportsman before the formal evening that follows. In Scotland, in the shooting season, dinner is often as late as nine, or even half-past nine; and in the long northern twilight candles are seldom needed before you sit down. The transformation in the appearance of the company when lights are brought in is sometimes startling. The rough garb of the sportsman has been exchanged for the habiliments of civilization, and the women are resplendent in jewels and lace. They take their finest diamonds to the wilds, and there is a peculiar fascination about the splendor and luxury of an aristocratic dinner, after the hardships and excitement of the forest and the moor.

The anglers have had more quiet pleasures, but they too boast at night of their successes, and the table groans under the results of the achievements of the day.

Partridge-shooting begins on the 1st of September, and is less arduous than grouse-shooting, and more of an English than a Scottish sport. Pheasants are not killed till October 1. This amusement also is principally a southern one, but every county in England has its pheasant preserves. The battues are enormous, and the covers like chicken yards. Game-keepers, indeed, are little more than stock-farmers, so far as pheasants are concerned; and many of the earnest shooters despise this phase of sport. The English themselves never call it " hunting;" they speak only of " shooting " pheasants. I should say butchering; for the pheasants are sold.

This is a feature of English sport that I never

ceased to wonder at. These noblemen and gentlemen with their hundreds of thousands of acres and their hundreds of thousands of income, their estates and castles and retainers, their crowds of aristocratic guests—nearly all sell their game. Now and then they send a friend a brace of birds or a haunch of venison, but the game market is stocked by the nobility. To many of them it is a considerable source of revenue. I was once staying with a well-known nobleman while General Grant was President. I had been out with the shooters, and thought it would be pleasant to send the President a brace of pheasants from the spot where they had been killed. I mentioned to one of the guests that I meant to suggest this to our host, but he cautioned me not to commit the blunder. The matter was discussed by the entire party, and every man declared it would be improper to make the request. The game was marketable, and it would be indelicate to ask for it, even if I had shot the birds. Nobody seemed to think this strange. The high spirit of an aristocrat did not revolt at selling the game that his guests had killed; and the man who was lavish of his courtesies would have been amazed had I proposed he should pay this compliment to the head of a foreign State.

The devotion to sport that characterizes the English aristocracy is not elevating. It not only makes them indifferent to more serious occupations, taking the hereditary legislators from the affairs of state to which they are supposed to apply themselves, and often distracting them from their own more important interests; but the incessant practice is certainly brutalizing. To be forever planning and inflicting death and pain, even on animals, cannot be refining. The English nature is coarse in itself, but sport renders it still more so. They say, indeed, that they shoot and kill and torture because all this is necessary in order to procure food. But butchering is also necessary, yet gentlemen do not select the shambles for their pastimes. The Frenchman's criticism was fair. "Let us go and kill something," is the Englishman's idea of pleasure; and it is a coarse one. An American soldier once said something like this at an English table in my hearing, and one of the company insinuated that the sentiment was maudlin. But the American, who had been in forty battles, replied: "Oh! I believe in killing nothing but men."

Like everything else in England, this pleasure is a matter of privilege. Game is strictly preserved for the great. The unprivileged man may not carry a gun. Every Englishman loves sport, the peasant as well as the peer, but poaching is a criminal offence; and the poor man is sent for two months, six months, even a year, to gaol, for doing what gives the rich man his keenest gratification. Five thousand committals for poaching are made every year in England alone. The landlord is the magistrate, and decides upon the punishment after convicting of the crime. In this country of privilege, there is property even in the air; and the peasant who has no farm, no house, and no hope of ever owning either, no amusement, often no meat, may not shoot the rabbit that roots up his garden, or the wild bird that flies over the moor.

Nothing can be more fascinating for those who are fond of the pastime than the methods of aristocratic athletic pleasure; nothing more elaborate and imposing than its appliances and appurtenances. God's uplands and valleys themselves are the playground of the nobility. The broad domains, the stretching moors, the thick coverts, the lofty mountains, the purple heath-covered hills, rolling and billowy, like the waves of the sea, and, like them, extending to the horizon, are all reserved unbroken and undisturbed, for the amusement of the aristocracy; these are the stage on which the great disport themselves. When across some scene of stately natural grandeur or bewitching cultivated grace there passes a company of the masters of the soil, issuing perhaps from a great castle hoary with age and famous in history, with their guests and retainers, their horses and hounds, and guns and game, bent on exhilarating, manly pleasure; surrounded with all that makes life splendid and gay—one cannot but admire the taste and luxury and magnificence that come from centuries of privilege and generations used to caste.

But at the same moment another procession of starving, houseless hinds, a million in number, is marching to the almshouse.

## XXVII.

### THE ACCESSIONS.

I ONCE made a bet with a high-born dame that not fifty of the English peerages were two hundred years old. She was the granddaughter of earls on both sides of the house, and insisted that my remark was mere republican raillery. So we agreed to leave the decision to her cousin, a vice-chamberlain, and of course an authority. He pronounced that in one sense I was right. If we considered the titles by which the peers are now known, the old ones are as few as I had declared, but there are still others in existence lost in the promotions to which their wearers have later attained. As I had bet with a lady I paid without a protest, and she rewarded me with an invitation to Oakley Park, the seat of Earl Bathurst, which Pope celebrated in the line:

"Who plants like Bathurst, and who builds like Boyle."

The peerage indeed would have been small by this time but for the accessions which it constantly receives. There were seventeen new lords created the last year I spent in England. Politics is the principal avenue that leads to the House of Lords. But though the Prime Minister makes noblemen by the score, only one premier in the last hundred years has given himself a peerage before the close of his career. Lord Beaconsfield could not wait so long, and seized the prize in advance. He also conferred the Order of the Garter on himself and took the office of Lord Privy Seal, which gave him precedence over all but five people in the kingdom, of less than royal degree. Sir Robert Walpole and Lord John Russell both took their promotion when they ceased to be premiers. Sir Robert Peel, the younger Pitt, and Charles James Fox remained commoners, but they all died young for English statesmen; as did also Canning. The widow of Canning, however, was made a viscountess. Lord Beaconsfield, on the contrary, made his wife a peeress long before he put on a coronet himself. Like most of the premiers, he felt that the House of Commons was his proper place, but the glitter of the gew-gaw was too much for him, and after a while he laid his hand upon an earldom. The wonder was he did not make himself a duke, for there was no one to say him nay. Doubtless had he remained in power, he would have mounted to the highest step in the ladder of the peerage, and donned the strawberry leaves.

The demand for promotion is very openly made. A political adherent who thinks his services entitle him to the reward has no hesitancy in presenting his claim. The late Sir Francis Goldsmid narrated to me in detail the persistent efforts his father made for this sort of recognition. Sir Isaac Goldsmid was one of the most prominent Jewish gentlemen in the kingdom; he had served, not only his party, but the country, faithfully and liberally, and advanced large sums to the Government in critical emergencies. He was extremely anxious for a title, but a peerage was out of the question, and he had a long struggle before Lord Palmerston consented to make him a baronet. This was forty-five years ago, and not until last year was a Jew created a peer; the head of the Rothschilds was then elevated to the House of Lords. Long before this the financial importance of the great Hebrew family had secured them nobility in nearly every other European state, but the Rothschilds were not satisfied till their wealth had bought them admission to the British House of Lords.

For these foreign titles, which the Continental courts do not scruple to bestow on successful bankers and others in trade, are not much esteemed in England. They confer no precedence there, and are not recognized at court. The bearers must obtain especial license from Her Majesty to use either arms or title, though they sometimes put the latter on their cards without authority. Not long ago there were two of these gentlemen living in England, well known and respected—Baron Worms and Baron Stern. The latter was made a viscount by some European sovereign, whereupon the wits remarked: "This will give him precedence of—Baron Worms."

Some years ago I congratulated a subordinate member of Mr. Gladstone's government upon being made a privy councillor, but the ambition of the placeman was far from appeased. He told me that his eldest son, then an Eton boy of twelve or thirteen years, had said to him: "Papa, if they offer you a peerage, be sure not to refuse it. Remember me." The boy and his father had evidently set their hearts on the same prize. The aspiring commoner has since become a peer, so that the son is satisfied; and the father, then a strong Radical, is now a Tory of the Tories.

In 1871 the Queen created the rich and charitable Miss Burdett-Coutts a baroness in her own right; a recognition of moral excellence never made before in the history of the British aristocracy. But even in this case the wealth was as indispensable as the individual worth. Lady Burdett-Coutts might have emulated the virtues of all the Saints in the Calendar, but if poverty had been on the list of her merits, she could not have entered the English peerage. Indeed, had Her Majesty foreseen that celibacy was not to be included, the wealthy philanthropist would certainly have remained a commoner. It was because there could be no successor that the sovereign was pleased to dispense her favor. The lady married, however, at the mature age of sixty-five, and the Queen was indignant at this violation of the implied contract; although it was certain the baroness would never transmit her honors to an heir.

Wealth has always been held an essential qualification in the candidates for the aristocracy, and many of those otherwise fitted for the promotion have failed of it because of the lack of this indispensable attribute. The great soldiers had to receive pensions and sometimes estates with their peerages, to enable them to maintain their dignity; and at one time the politicians also reckoned pelf as well as promotion among their perquisites, but of late years the public feeling would not have sanctioned such a disposition of the public moneys.

The Speaker of the House of Commons is the first Commoner in the Kingdom, and always receives a peerage when he resigns, that he may not step back into the ranks. The Speaker of the House of Lords is the Lord Chancellor; if not already a peer he is always promoted before he ascends the woolsack, and remains noble, of course, with his family forever. The greatest of the lawyers is thus always a peer; but the most successful of his brethren are never ennobled, unless they have amassed sufficient fortunes to compete with inherited splendor.

Physicians may never arrive at the peerage. The slur of the older days, when barbers were surgeons, remains; and the most eminent medical men who illustrate the English name to-day, though they save the lives of princes and lessen the sufferings of humanity, are never rewarded with more than a baronetcy. The English doctors take their pay with every visit, and the saying is that no man who has held out his hand for a fee can ever be made an English peer. Yet many of the nobility have held out their hands—for bribes.

The great brewers, however, nearly all attain to the aristocratic degree. Malt seems to possess a peculiar patrician quality, though no man of letters or purely literary genius, except Tennyson, has ever received a coronet. The blood of the Basses and Alsops and Guinnesses may become "blue," but that of Browning and Thackeray and Froude remains plebeian.

After politics and money, marriage is the key that unlocks the august portals of the aristocracy with greatest ease. The nobility may marry whom they please, and their wives will be peeresses; their (legitimate) children are all in the succession, even if born of dairy-maids. Many of the wives of the lords are from the middle class. A rich heiress can buy a coronet any day. There are marchionesses now living whose fortunes fresh from trade saved the ancient estates of aristocracy from the hammer; while ladies with the odor of tobacco about their garments have penetrated into patrician families and shone in the most exclusive spheres. The taint disappears at the entrance. They leave the shop entirely behind when once they are initiated.

I knew a countess who dropped her H's, yet she visited the daughters of dukes. I discussed her once with a high-born associate of her later years, who pretended to believe she was American in origin. "No, no, Lady Charlotte," I replied, "the H's prove her nationality;"—and Lady Charlotte unwillingly admitted that the evidence was irrefutable.

Of late years, American beauties and fortunes have often found their way into the aristocracy; and the Queen can count among her nobler subjects at least half a score who began life as republicans.

The stage has furnished peeresses from the days when Miss Farren became Countess of Derby down to a Countess of Essex that I knew, who had been a public singer, and whose manners were as courtly and her assemblies as crowded as those of the De Veres. Miss O'Neill, the tragedian, became Lady Becher, and was living until lately, charming and respected. The Countess Waldegrave in her youth accompanied her father, Braham, the tenor, at his concerts, at the same houses which were afterwards proud to welcome her as a guest; and there is a woman of title and fashion in London to-day, whom a famous wit assured me he saw enter Brighton in tights and on a camel. Now she entertains sovereigns. Every one will remember the ancestress of the St. Albans who sold oranges in the pit to Charles II., and her virtue afterward to the same customer at a higher price.

Beauty has always won the favor of the British peers. The eldest son, or the man in possession, can afford to please his taste; and doubtless the handsome looks of many of the nobility are due to the beautiful women who have recruited its ranks so largely. The illegitimate children of sovereigns have been ennobled, down to and including the last reign, and in the present day young peers and heirs have sought mates in half a score of instances among those whose presence sullies any society they enter.

The blue blood does not seem to curdle at the contact, for the grandest of English peers welcome to their ancestral homes the brewers and bankers, the tailors and tobacconists, who, as soon as they become noble, look down as superciliously on plebeians as any descendant of peer or paramour. A stroke of the wand of Cinderella's godmother turned vermin into decorated lackeys fit to go to court; and the flunkeys did not forget their rat-hole more readily than these transformed aristocrats their early obscurity. Blood will tell; and their blood is noble—now.

## XXVIII.

### LITERATURE AND THE LORDS.

It is the fashion to say that in these days the barriers of rank are broken down, that literary reputation is a social passport, and genius opens all doors; that the aristocracy itself has entered the lists and recognized the equality of poets and philosophers with its highest members. But nothing can be more fallacious than this opinion. The lords open their doors to men and women of parts, it is true, but the purpose is to amuse themselves, not to do honor to literature. In old times they had their jesters and their bards, to while away the time or to chronicle their deeds. Froissart and Ben Jonson did little more, in their eyes. So the Queen still keeps a poet laureate to celebrate the births and marriages of her progeny, and duchesses have authors and actors at their parties to entertain their guests, as they have music and ice-cream.

The geniuses would like to believe, because they are sometimes invited to dinner, or even to a country-house, that the feeling of the aristocracy is changed; but let one of them ask to marry the daughter of a duke and he will discover how wide is the gulf that separates them. Let him presume in any way too far upon the notice that he thinks is a friendship, and he will be dropped with as little ceremony as if his lordship were dismissing a footman. The people of letters are admitted or invited to-day, and forgotten or ignored to-morrow. They may be in society for a while, they are never of it; and if they no longer wait in the ante-room as Johnson did at Chesterfield House, they must make themselves either serviceable or agreeable if they expect to stay upstairs. They know this very well, though they don't always tell it, and the more dignified ones keep aloof from the great world. Dickens was invited to Windsor to play in private theatricals before the Queen, but refused to go, because he could not be received as a gentleman. Others, however, are content to follow in the train where their wives are seldom placed at all, or to sit at the bottom of the table, as really now as in the days of Temple and Swift, below the salt.

I know that all this will be denied. A well-known wit, himself a middle-class man, who was much invited because of his learned gossip and his talent for repartee, wrote pages in the *Quarterly Review* to prove that a man who has attained distinction in any walk of life is received on a footing of equality by the aristocracy. But the assertion is preposterous. Taine and Laugel, the two acutest critics of English life in later years, assert the contrary. Gladstone and Thackeray constantly proclaim the existence of the distinction that I describe. Laugel declares: "For the middle-man, for the peasant, for the shop-keeper, even for the Radical, the lord is not a man like another." Lord Houghton, the most liberal of aristocrats, wrote: "There are barriers in our social life which no individual will or power can throw down. You cannot bring into close sympathetic communion the operative poor and the inoperative rich, any more in intellectual than in physical relations." To illustrate this he describes a passage between Lady Ashburton and Thackeray. The novelist had been much invited by the aristocrat, but there came a difference between them and a discontinuance of the social relations. Houghton says that Thackeray was discourteous. After a while, however, the peeress, as the grander personage, made an advance. She sent the literary man a card to dinner, and he replied with a pictorial acceptance, representing himself on his knees at her ladyship's feet, while she was heaping coals of fire on his head from an ornamented brazier. After this, says Lord Houghton, she was always very kind to Thackeray and his family.

Mrs. Carlyle tells of a journey she and her great husband made to Scotland in the train of this same Lady Ashburton, who took them along indeed, but in a separate compartment, as she would her lackey or her lap-dog. Carlyle, it is true, sometimes was sent in to dinner at the head of the company, but so was Sara Bernhardt, in my time; and in each instance the distinction was an impertinence. It was not because the author or the actor was considered above the nobility, but because they were not in the degrees at all. The forms which the aristocracy maintain among themselves are inapplicable with such outsiders, and the dramatic or literary lions may in this way come to receive the place usually reserved for princes. If they were given a definite station in the line it would be more like a recognition of their quality. But nobody supposed the French artist was grander than duchesses because she walked in before them; and to-day if she went back to London, the houses where she once was welcomed, would be closed to her. The fashion is past.

Two or three men of letters have, it is true, maintained a permanent position in aristocratic society, but it is one neither lofty nor dignified. These are received not because of any personal distinction or position, not because they have written poetry or history or romance, but because they are men of agreeable manners and interesting information, used to the forms and relishing the frivolities of the great world—intellectual courtiers and time-servers. They are diners-out, though they don't dine lords in return; they haunt ball-rooms and race-courses and country-houses; but they are seldom seen at court. In the ordinary intercourse of society you might imagine that they belonged to the sphere in which they seem to move, but the moment the great question of rank is raised, they fall back to their own place; everybody precedes them and passes by them, and if matters of privilege are discussed, they are necessarily and of course ignored.

But the nobility, it is said, is itself engaged in literature; and the lords, and the ladies, too, do dabble a little in literature. Lord Mahon, afterwards Lord Stanhope, wrote a dreary history; the Duke of Argyll has discussed science, and the late Duke of Somerset religion, in a manner quite abnormal in dukes, but their labors would have attracted little attention in persons of lower degree. A dozen or more lords and lordlings have written books of travel or memoirs, with the assistance of their doctors, or tutors, or secretaries; and one or two titled dames have put their names to really readable romances; while, as the courts of law can testify, the quality contribute gossip and scandal at a guinea an item to the society journals, and an editor has been sent to jail for the libels that a countess supplied.

But these caprices of the aristocracy never lower them in the eyes of their equals or inferiors. A duke or a countess may write books and not lose caste, just as some of them play in private theatricals or sing at concerts for charity; the Duke of Edinburgh even plays the violin in public in the orchestra. But all this is very different from belonging to the trade. Dukes drive the coach to Brighton, and I have seen a viscount touch his hat and take a tip from an unknown passenger, as he put a portmanteau into the boot. But for all that, no one considered him the fellow of a genuine Jehu. So it is with literature.

The Duke of Argyll is looked upon as *par excellence* the literary peer. While I was in London he presided at a Press Fund dinner. His speech was full of condescension and consideration for the literary guild. He applauded the merits of these worthy members of the middle class, declared that they should be protected, and supported and encouraged; and altogether spoke of them about as a Congressman here might discuss the occupants of tenement-houses or broken-down cobblers deserving charity.

The literary people were of the same mind as his Grace. They were delighted to get a duke to talk thus to them; to teach them their duty, to preside at their dinner and send them a couple of guineas for their fund. The spirit of the jester still lingers. Thackeray himself tells how proud he was to walk down Pall Mall between dukes. Sir Thomas Erskine May, who has lived all his life among lords, devotes pages of his Constitutional History of England to glorifying and upholding the influence of the aristocracy. Yet Thackeray satirized the foibles of the people he considered his betters with a lash as cutting as Juvenal's, and Erskine May describes in detail the corruptions and meannesses, the bargains and sales, the tricks and devices by means of which the peerage has been recruited and maintained. The newspapers follow the lead of the poets and novelists and historians. Pages of every journal are devoted to descriptions of feasts to which newspaper writers are never asked, and to details of the life and pursuits of the most ordinary characters who happen to have title and rank, from Princes of the Blood down to city knights and Companions of the Bath.

Everybody in England knows how a lord is made; that barbers may become Lord Chancellors and brewers get baronies; that political service or trickery, or wealth obtained often by questionable means, can secure that nobility which is denied to science and letters and art. Yet Froude and Leckey and May uphold the system, and journalists with more power than any duke in the peerage, prostrate themselves in their columns at the mention of a lord. Nine-tenths of the literary men in England feel honored when asked to the tables of persons with less education or character or ability than themselves.

The people who use the pen, indeed, do more for the continuance of the aristocratic system and the development of its pernicious influence than any other class in the community. They spread the doctrines and intensify the sentiments which support an institution more hostile to the greatest good of the greatest number than any other that exists in civilized society. If the men of letters fought the lords, the lords would succumb. But the men of letters serve and follow the lords, and the aristocracy flaunt their insolence in the face of the world, and take these intellectual superiors in their train to proclaim their magnificence, to illuminate their feasts, and to celebrate the splendor they may not share. These deserve the place they accept. They recall a description I long ago read of a Russian serf carefully holding the horses for his master, who stood on the shafts, while he horse-whipped the slave.

One of the most famous English writers of the century told me that he had once been very intimate with Motley, the historian. They were fellow-laborers in the same field; but after the American was made a Minister the British author held aloof. Motley, he said, was now in another sphere; he lived in the aristocratic circle where English men of letters do not belong. He evidently thought the diplomatist would look down on the literary class, and he recognized the distance that rank had put between himself and his old associate.

## XXIX.

### THE LONDON SEASON.

The season depends upon Parliament, and Parliament depends upon sport. The fashionable world is composed very largely of those connected with either the House of Lords or the House of Commons; and when Parliament meets, their families come up to town. For the nobility live in the country, their homes are on their estates, and their town-houses are only for sojourn when they happen to be in London. The great world does not begin its whirl till politics summons the important members to transact the business of the nation. In February, usually in the second week, after the best of the hunting is over, the Queen—that is, the Prime Minister—calls her "lords and gentlemen" together. Then the fashionable season begins.

The people connected with the government, the diplomatic corps, those of the gentry who have no large estates, the lawyers and literary people, and others who live by their exertions, all these are in town for the most part from November, with an interval of a fortnight at Christmas. They make a very pleasant and intimate society among themselves: small but accessible, and often much more delightful than the more pompous and pretentious circle that comes only with Parliament.

From February until Easter is another pleasant period. London is not yet crowded. Many families do not leave the country so soon. The rush has not begun. There are yet no court-balls nor concerts, and the veterans make a point of attending the levees and drawing-rooms at this time, so as to avoid the mobs that crowd to court later on. The ante-paschal season is perhaps the most agreeable part of the London year. There are few dances in Lent, and not so many of the formal receptions which nobody wants to attend and yet everybody attends. There are incessant dinners, but many of them are small; there are occasional theatre parties, and numerous five-o'clock teas.

But just as people begin to get used to each other, and fall into the habit of meeting two or three times a week those whom they really want to see—Easter intervenes. Parliament is adjourned, and everybody who has a house in the country goes to it. Large country-house parties are made, and the world of politics and fashion deserts London. Those who have neither country-houses nor country invitations would be lonely in town, and they run off to the Continent for a fortnight, or to Brighton, or some other resort of forlorn, houseless, fashionable wanderers.

After Easter the full tide sets in, everybody is up. The great houses are all open; the park is full in the afternoon; the Row is crowded every morning with a thousand horsewomen, the finest in the world, and the Englishwomen look better in the saddle than anywhere else. Lunches are frequent, dinners innumerable. Forty people often sit at one sumptuous board, and the overflow sometimes reaches to side tables; clever people, if not of too high rank, contend for these cosy corners, where they can choose their partners. Balls now begin, to the sorrow of unfortunate chaperones and the delight of the debutantes. The Queen's drawing-rooms are crowded. Politics are everywhere discussed. Theatres and operas are abandoned by people of fashion; for you cannot dine at eight o'clock and go to the play the same night; while the opera has for years been given up to those who like music, and to strangers and others who fancy it is the mode, because it was so half a century ago.

But the whirl lasts only four or five weeks, when Whitsuntide comes; and then another recess, and more than half the world flits again to the country, which by this time is enchanting. I used at first to find these constant interruptions to the round of society very provoking; just as one got in the swim there was a gate or a dike, and a halt;

but after some years I liked the fashion too. The lilacs and laburnums, the hawthorne and the gorse are all in their glory about Whitsuntide, and those who have ever seen the resplendent beauty of the flowering trees and meads of England, or heard the music of the nightingale and the lark, the blackbird and the thrush in May or early June, they know the exquisite charm of sound and color and fragrance that permeates the landscape, the refreshment of brain and sense that comes with the balmy atmosphere of this soft and gracious time.

There are not so many large parties to the country at Whitsuntide as at Easter. The recess is shorter, and those who go down to their estates sometimes go for the pleasure of seeing them in their vernal garment of tender green and variegated border, or to rest before the great plunge into the vortex of fashion after their return.

You come back, usually, late in May. It is now the height of the season. The country is never so attractive in its loveliness, but many of the owners of great estates assured me they had never seen their homes in June. They possess great gardens of geraniums, roseries in which no land can rival England, lawns and pastures and groves and glades delicious in verdure beyond those of any country on earth; but since childhood these slaves of the world have never known what it was to look on their own landscapes and enjoy the principal beauty of their own properties at the season when their natural glories culminate. You must be in town in June, if you are in the world.

You must go to late dinners and later balls. You must breathe the hot atmosphere of Parliament, and the still more stifling air at court. You must be clad in the stiff garments that etiquette prescribes for every hour; you must devote yourself to a round of visits and entertainments which would be most acceptable in dreary winter, but now distract you from delights that are rare in England because of the climate. At this moment, when the climate and the country are alike Saturnian, you forsake the country and come up to town. For so fashion decrees. Or rather so the sportsmen determine; the men will not abandon their guns and their game in the autumn and winter, and this leaves only the spring and summer for town. And in England, society, like everything else, is ruled by the men. The women only exist to give them pleasure and do them service; to marry them, to rear their children, to preside over their homes, to decorate their entertainments. What the men want is always done, and the women submit, as a matter of course.

But since they must be in town in summer, the English make the best of the necessity. Half their amusements are out of doors. First there is the Derby day, about the last of May or the first of

June. In some years this is the fashion, in others, not; but Parliament always adjourns for the race; and the people who live in the streets leading to Epsom, hang carpets over their balconies and invite their friends to look at the returning crowds. On the 4th of June there is Commencement at Eton, and a boat-race by the boys, to which swarms of smart people go down.

Then there are cricket matches between the Lords and the Commons, between Oxford and Cambridge, between Eton and Harrow. These are held at a pleasure-ground called "Lord's" in the outskirts of London, and are very high fashion indeed. The great folk send their largest carriages down the night before, and the enclosure is lined three rows deep. Next day they drive down in landaus, broughams, and victorias, and mount the drags or coaches in their gayest gowns and highest beavers, to watch the game. They lunch on the carriages and get back in time for dinner.

Above all now is the time for garden parties. Chiswick is a delightful seat of the Duke of Devonshire on the banks of the Thames, which in some years he lends to the Prince of Wales on condition that His Highness gives two great breakfasts a season. The parties at Strawberry Hall are historical, as well as those at Sion House and Osterley, the parks of the Duke of Northumberland and the Dowager Duchess of Cleveland. The nearest of these is ten miles from London, but people think nothing of driving out and back between luncheon and dinner. Closer to town are the lodges of the Duke of Argyll and Lady Burdett-Coutts; and noblest of all, Holland House, with its memories more stately even than its architecture, and more unfading than its far-famed landscape and lawn. All these are thronged every season with people of highest rank and oldest name; as many statesmen and soldiers and diplomatists as butterflies of fashion, wits or belles, or dowagers or dandies. Even the Queen throws open the gardens of Buckingham Palace sometimes in July, and invites a few thousand of her greatest subjects to afternoon tea.

These garden parties are unique in effect and loveliness. The women wear costumes of the lightest fabrics and most delicate colors, appropriate in tint and texture for a ball; the men are the best dressed and the handsomest in the world; the lawns and trees and gardens make the most charming background; there are marquees and music, carpets spread here and there on the grass; sometimes an archery match or an alfresco play; sometimes Punch and Judy under the blossoms for the children. The scene is worthy of Watteau's daintiest pencil.

In the midst of all this comes Ascot week, when those who have invitations whirl down to the races which royalty attends in state. This makes another lull in the gayety, but only a lull; for it is now July and every one has too much to do. There are the Court balls and concerts; an Emperor, or a Shah, or a Czar is sure to arrive, whom some very grand personage must entertain, and everybody must go to see him, or say they have done so. Politics are at fever heat. Some important question is to be debated or settled in Parliament, and the world goes to the House of Lords for a night. Dinners at Richmond are popular at this period. People drive down in morning dress and boat on the Thames, or sit on the Terrace and look at the marvellous landscape which Turner painted but could not rival. They dine at the Star and Garter Inn, and drive back through the delicious glades of Richmond Park in the long twilight or the moonlight, or perhaps under a shower that touches every leaf with a more glistening green, yet hardly harms the most fragile garment of the gayest noble dame.

Wimbledon is the last of the *fêtes champêtres*. All the world goes to see the shooting by the Volunteers, and the lucky ones stop at one or two of the charming retreats that still linger along the road, hidden from the passer-by, who never suspects the exquisite charm of woodland and dell so near and yet concealed.

But the Lords, and the Commons too, begin to get restive as August approaches; for on the twelfth grouse-shooting begins. Arrangements are made for Scotland and the North; those who are ordered to Carlsbad or Kissingen for their sins, or their amusement, make ready to start. A few familiar faces are already missed. Here and there a great house is closed. There are not so many carriages in the Ring, not so many riders in the Row. Of a Sunday afternoon there are fewer light gowns on the seats in Hyde Park. The debates are more languid. The Minister announces what measures he must abandon for lack of time, and this "Massacre of the Innocents," as it is called, is a sure precursor of the end. Usually by the sacred 12th, all is over, and if by some strange fatality the Houses have not yet been prorogued, the world is gone; streets and halls are deserted; the gay and the great are scattered over mountain and moor, in Switzerland or the Highlands, shooting, or drinking the waters, or resting for their autumnal labors. The London season is at an end.

## XXX.

### ARISTOCRATIC INFLUENCE.

As a legislative body, the Peers must hereafter always yield when they are opposed by the will of a popular minister; but those are greatly mistaken who suppose that their sway is entirely past. On the outside of Parliament the Lords are still powerful if not paramount. In society, on their estates, in the hunting field, in the Church, the army, the press, the courts of law, their influence is prodigious.

In all the circles that make up English high society, aristocratic politics are predominant. What the Lords think and wish is all-important there. Nothing in this world can be more delightful or desirable for the fortunate few who possess it, than the position of the English aristocrats; and naturally they favor the political party which aims at retaining this position for them; or, rather, they lead and control, they constitute, and to a great degree compose it. At clubs and dinners and country houses, as well as in the newspapers controlled by those who frequent such places or aspire to do so, the tone of politics is generally very different from what prevails in less exclusive spheres. Public opinion often does not penetrate to the Peers, but their opinions always filter outward and downward. Every great lady in England is interested in the movements and measures of politics, and is acquainted with most of the prominent men, at least on her own side. Many are politicians themselves, and some have really been leaders, though as a rule only of personal cliques and for personal motives. They are, of course, conservative.

When Lord Beaconsfield returned from Berlin in 1878, having arrested the advance of Russia upon Constantinople, half a dozen duchesses met him at the railway station with salutations and flowers, to indicate their partisanship. Later still there have been instances of women of rank attempting to influence the electors. It is not long since Lady Derby was openly accused of illegally soliciting votes on Lord Derby's estates. The first Lady Dilke, though only a baronet's wife, drove about London in an open carriage distributing favors when her husband was a candidate; and the part that an American aristocrat, Lady Randolph Churchill, took in the elections of 1885, is as well known here as in England.

All of which shows that the blandishments of rank are as potent with the tradesmen of Chelsea or the peasants of Woodstock, as with Prime Ministers. For it is not only the feminine charm that is irresistible, although Englishmen as a rule are very manly, and therefore very susceptible to womanly wiles; but had these ladies been simply the equals of those whom they sought to affect, their success would not have been achieved nor their effort made. It was arrogance and assumption of the most arrant sort. But the English like arrogance and assumption in their betters. They consider these qualities appropriate in those entitled to display them.

The aristocratic influence does not stop short at society, nor is it confined to elections. Wealth everywhere that is not inherited, whether acquired by manufactures or commerce or whatever means, seeks to bask in the favor of the nobility, is ambitious of their connection, craves admission to their company. The professions lean for their support on the higher orders. The lawyers, who manage the estates of the lords, and the physicians, who care for their bodies, are alike dependants of the aristocracy, and so regard themselves. The Church and the army have long been appurtenances of the great monopoly. The clergy are, for the most part, the creatures of lay patronage, and peculiarly connected with the landed interest; they everywhere cleave to power. Not until 1871 was purchase abolished in the army. Up to that date, the purchase of commissions was one of the especial and favorite means by which the aristocracy provided for its members and preserved its privileges. The army is to-day officered in a great degree by men who bought their rank, and expected when they did so to buy their promotion.

Even in the courts of law the influence of the aristocracy is apparent. A lord may sit on the bench beside a judge, though often he is a notorious violator of the law. If a drunken marquis or a rowdy viscount is brought before a magistrate, he is usually treated with servile deference, a fine is meted out to him for the offence which in a humbler culprit would be punished with imprisonment, and my lord is bowed graciously out of court. The English are fond of proclaiming the incorruptible character of their judiciary, and of late years judges have hardly ever been bought with money; but social influences have repeatedly affected the conduct and the decisions of the courts. In the famous Tichborne case the whole pressure of society was brought to bear upon judge and advocate, till, to the disgrace of the profession and the bench, the barrister threw up his brief and deserted his client when the case was only half tried, and two judges in succession ruled so notoriously to the prejudice of the accused that both the press and public opinion proclaimed a disapproval.

In the case of the will of a late Lord Chancellor, a decision, manifestly in violation of law, was brought about by similar influences. The testimony of the daughter of Lord St. Leonards was received as to the language of a will in her own favor, though the original will was lost. There was, in fact, no proof that the will had ever been made, except the evidence of the interested party; yet the judge decided that a document reversing all the ordinary rules of English descent should be accepted, though it had never been in court. But high society was hostile to the regular heir.

The influence of the aristocracy upon literature and the press is too important a theme to be discussed in a paragraph. But there are many of the learned and intellectual men of England so affected by the splendor and pageantry of rank that their reason is subdued by their imagination; or else they are so constituted by nature that they prefer stability to progress. Since so much has been achieved under aristocratic rule they are averse to change, and remain indifferent to the misery which must exist so long as the great disparity of condition continues.

The tradesmen in the cities and smaller towns are supported by the aristocracy; the farmers in the country are their tenants and dependants; of course, these follow the lead of their masters and superiors.

The hinds, as they are still called, the helots on the estates, are as stolid and brutish a race as any peasantry in the world, and seem, like the slaves at the South before emancipation, content with their condition, because they have never known or conceived any other. They are bred to suppose that what they see is the natural order of things, and that change is not only wrong but impossible; that their lot is ordained of God, as inevitable as death, and deliverance as far off as the stars. The parson preaches this doctrine for religion; the squire lays it down as the law; for the squire is also the Justice of the Peace, the highest and often the only officer of the law the laborer ever sees. Law, religion, rank, power, all are on one side; and the wretch with his shilling a day and his family to support lives near the palace of his master, and rots and drinks, or starves and dies, ignorant of the possibility of improvement, and submissive—they say.

I remember discussing the permanency of English institutions with a man who had been in half the Governments of England during the last fifty years. He expressly invited my opinions, and I spoke freely. I said that of course the aristocracy and the upper classes were content with their condition, and even with the general state of affairs; that the middle class—comprising those who live by the aristocracy—the tradesmen, the domestic servants, and the farmers, and higher still, those who aspire to enter the aristocracy, or, at least, to associate with it, were unwilling to disturb that order which is their support and their pride; but when the class below all these is reached, the manufacturing working class and the agricultural laborer —eight millions at least in numbers—I doubted whether content was universal or whether, if they had the power, they would use it to maintain either Crown or Lords. It was then that he replied with the remark I have quoted before: "Every Englishman is at heart a lackey. We all want something above us; something to kotow to."

He admitted that the manufacturing working people were radical, and perhaps revolutionary, in their ideas; but he thought the hinds on the estates preferred to have superiors; that the feudal feeling with them was still uppermost; that they were satisfied. Stolid, it seems to me they are, but not satisfied; and when they get some notion that a different life for them is possible, when they discover that their class in other countries exerts an influence, I would not answer for their submissiveness. The lackeys may be taken from this class, but not all the class are lackeys. The President of the Poor Law Board, the highest authority on these matters in England, informed me that there are a million of paupers in the kingdom, wretches without a particle of means, supported by the State. It is impossible that the contrast between this worse than poverty and the opulence and luxury of others should not sometimes present itself to the stupidest mind. The very week after this conversation the agricultural disturbances of 1870 occurred, and the movement led by Joseph Arch; and all England was anxious for months lest the helots should rise. To-day they have the ballot.

## GLADSTONE—THE ICONOCLAST.

The great antagonist of Aristocracy in England at the present time is William Ewart Gladstone; yet he began his career as a Tory and High-Churchman. One of Macaulay's early essays was a Whig attack on a manifesto by a young man whom the reviewer called "The Rising Hope of the Stern and Unbending Tories." The book was Gladstone's defence of "The State in its Relations with the Church." To-day the Tory has passed beyond the position even of the Whigs, and left them far to the rear. In both Church and State they are the drag and he is the leader—as the coach rolls rapidly down the hill of Revolution—the Tories say.

His transition has been gradual. No statesman in history has grown more steadily or furnished a finer instance of evolution. For years he was simply the great financier of his party; he looked little to the revolutionary or progressive politics that were developing around him. But, as the old leaders like Sir Robert Peel, Lord Palmerston, and the last Lord Derby passed away, and Lord Russell became decrepit and finally senile, two younger men stepped into the arena, grander figures in English politics than any since the days of Pitt and Fox, and one, at least, destined to leave a deeper impress on the history of his country than even those giants of the Napoleonic day.

In 1869, when I first went to England, Disraeli and Gladstone were the acknowledged chiefs of the two great political camps. One had worked his way up by the adroitest use of all the arts of policy and personal address, by attacking his friends and deserting his chiefs at opportune crises, by truckling to the prejudices and trading on the fears of a powerful order; above all, by the aid of an intense selfishness that was able to perceive its ends from afar, and to subject principle and even passion to its purposes; the very Mephistopheles and Machiavelli of modern politics; mocking, insincere, indifferent, so far as others were concerned; persistent, devoted, all-grasping in his own designs; grand in his power to compel a race that he despised and an aristocracy that despised him, to do his bidding. The other was a religious zealot, an intense thinker, and yet a practical man; full of love for the church and saturated with scholarly veneration for the past; with all the inborn reverence of an Englishman for whatever is established, and the awe of a middle-class man for the aristocracy: yet impelled by the combined force of his own energies and ambitions, and the tremendous vigor of his ever-expanding intellectual convictions, as well as by the influence of the iconoclastic and reforming spirit of the time—that penetrated and finally permeated him—till he turned upon the institutions he had loved the best, and like one inspired by the Fates, attacked and destroyed what he had been all his life upholding and defending. He was at the head of a brilliant band of ardent thinkers and earnest patriots, some of them doubtless crude or *doctrinaire*, impractical and over-zealous; others inclining to the extreme of caution, yet representing the element in English statesmanship which at that time had accomplished whatever had been achieved by or for the English people since the downfall of the Stuarts.

The first gage of battle was the Irish Church. Gladstone was made Prime Minister that he might overthrow that relic of the ancient alliance of Church and State which he had once written a book to defend. The religious enthusiast, the early apostle of Establishment, led the Whigs and the Radicals in their assault on the Church, while the political adventurer, the renegade from Liberalism, the foreigner in blood and belief, was the champion of the ecclesiastical hierarchy, of the aristocracy, and in reality, of the court. Their rivalry lasted till the death of Beaconsfield. Only one of these men could be Prime Minister so long as both were living.

Gladstone's convictions, his enemies say, have always been easily changed when the motive was strong; and it must be admitted that his conversions have often been seasonable. Any one who had studied his career could easily have predicted his course in the Irish emergency. He was certain to yield when the enemy became irresistible; to lead those to victory whose victory he had himself opposed. Circumstances, however, make potent arguments. When the political necessity is pressing, the political vision becomes clearer, and emergency often compels to a course that if the emergency did not exist might be unadvisable. It should be remembered, too, that Gladstone's progress has always been in one direction. After he once set out towards Liberalism he has never been a backslider. When he could not proceed as far as he wished he has neither retreated nor recanted. Whatever the inducement, whether of hope or fear, he never returns to his idols.

He has been accused of a jesuitical tendency, of a disposition to find arguments in favor of acts after the acts have been performed; and it is certain that when good logic was not at his disposal he has sometimes resorted to sophistries unworthy of the preacher of purity and Christianity infused into politics. Two notable instances of this occurred while I was in England.

One was generally known as the Ewelme scandal.

The living of Ewelme is in the gift of the Prime Minister, but a provision of law requires the incumbent to be a member of the University of Oxford. Mr. Gladstone had a favorite who was a Cambridge man, and, that he might receive the coveted preferment, this clergyman was first made a member of Oxford and then immediately promoted to the position reserved for Oxford men. The proceeding provoked much harsh criticism, and the Christian statesman certainly laid himself open to the charge of evading the law for personal purposes.

The other case affected the judiciary. Only judges who have sat in certain courts are eligible for appointment to the Judicial Committee of the Privy Council, a Court of Appeal of the highest dignity and consequence. Its members must be selected from the bench, so that their judicial experience may tell in their new position. But Mr. Gladstone appointed his Attorney-General, Sir Robert Collier, to a judgeship for two days, and then bestowed on him the preferment intended exclusively for the bench. These acts speak for themselves. His enemies not unnaturally proclaimed that the man who talked so loudly of truth and purity had poisoned the fountains of both religion and justice, and carried his favoritism in spite of law into the Church and the Courts.

These traits may not be omitted from the portrait, but it is pleasant to turn to other features of his character and other incidents in his career. The long list of his achievements in behalf of progress should not be forgotten in America. During his first two administrations Gladstone accomplished more than any other English statesman since Cromwell has even attempted in the way of overthrowing abuses and reforming institutions. He not only disestablished the Irish Church and renovated the system of Irish tenancy; he introduced the ballot into England, he abolished purchase in the army, he extended education, he brought about the recent extension of the franchise. He has opened the way for the admission of the poorest and humblest Englishman to the highest political rights, and made inevitable the modification and eventual abolition of the firmest-rooted wrongs and the unfairest privileges. Whenever equality, not only of position, but of opportunity, is established in England, Gladstone will be looked upon as the John the Baptist, the fore-runner of the Messiah.

In foreign matters he has championed the oppressed of many lands. More than a quarter of a century ago he directed attention to the atrocities of King Bomba of Naples, and assisted in precipitating the downfall of that royal monster; and in this way pioneered the coming of the kingdom of Italy. His eloquent utterances after the Bulgarian massacres, the tremendous invectives he poured on Turkish depravity, are not yet forgotten, and undoubtedly were the chief weapon that struck the cynical friend of the Turk, Lord Beaconsfield, from power.

For in foreign affairs Gladstone has never hesitated to manifest a spirit almost unexampled in the statesmen of any country or time. Hardly ever has republican or monarchist dared to set his country right, when she was in the wrong, before the world; to confess for her the wrong, to withdraw her from a false position, to emulate the gospel spirit, and carry Christianity into politics on so grand a scale. The retrocession of the Ionian islands, the similar policy in South Africa, the determination not to do evil in India that good might come; the refusal to resist the encroachments of Russia by perfidious or iniquitous means, or to support the Turk in evil practices because those practices might tend to the benefit of England—these are remarkable instances of what I mean. The submission to arbitration of the question whether England had done wrong in the Alabama matter, was a step of the same character; while the expression of regret for the injury inflicted was a humiliation that no statesman ever before in history put upon his country willingly. Some will call the act sublime; but there were many Englishmen who considered it pusillanimous. It was not pusillanimous, for it was not extorted by fear; and it tended to produce a cordial sentiment between the two countries that nothing else could have evoked.

Gladstone went through a storm of obloquy and condemnation on this account. I was in England still, and could watch his course. Public sentiment was so violent that at times the representatives of the United States felt its influence in their personal and social relations, and when the famous "Indirect Claims" were presented, the nations stood on the verge of war. Americans at home hardly appreciated the intensity of the British sentiment, but those in England, especially if they had access to official or important circles, knew the depth of the feeling. The press and Parliament were almost unanimous in their bitterness and their unfairness. But Mr. Gladstone never swerved from his intention or his effort to carry out what he had promised. His loyalty and the skilful diplomacy of Secretary Fish and General Schenck, which has never been recognized as it deserves, brought the two peoples through a crisis of no ordinary character.

The foreign policy of Mr. Gladstone has never met the general approbation of his countrymen: his genius does not shine in the sphere of diplomacy. Certainly the result in Egypt was not one to be proud of. The bombardment of Alexandria was a reproach to the English nation, and an outrage on the civilization of the age—punished in the same region and the same decade by the disasters of the Soudan and the massacre of Gordon. In each of his earlier administrations Mr. Gladstone so mismanaged his foreign relations that they undoubtedly contributed in each instance to his downfall. He offended unnecessarily the spirit of the English nation, humiliated its pride, and seemed, at least, to ignore its interests.

And this cannot be attributed to his lieutenants. Though he had at the head of his foreign department a man utterly without force or originality, it was not Lord Granville's fault that the tangle was so bad. For Gladstone is always master in his own cabinet. He controls and directs absolutely. His will is law. He dictates the general policy and decides every detail of importance, and his subordinates must yield or leave. His party too has followed, as well as his cabinet. No man has more absolutely swayed the nation when he was at its head. It was he who determined on Disestablishment in Ireland, and Arbitration with the United States; on Peace or War with Russia, and Africa, and Egypt, and America. It is he who made the coalition with Parnell; it is he who decided that Ireland must have a Parliament. Not Bismarck, not the first Napoleon, was more of an autocrat.

His ablest subalterns are proud to serve under him, though they scowl at any other chief. When, after the Liberal defeat in 1874, he retired for a while from the leadership of the party, to a man they besought him to remain. And when, upon his refusal, Lord Hartington for a while was allowed to hold the reins, Gladstone was still a disturbing element. Whenever for a night he appeared in Parliament, the nominal chief at once went into eclipse; and when at last his party returned to power, the country would hear of no one but him for Prime Minister. The Queen opposed him, but made herself and her weakness ridiculous by the opposition.

His personal popularity is prodigious; but, like all great men, he provokes the most violent animosities; not only among those who know him individually, but in the country at large. He is hated by the mass of the aristocracy with a bitterness almost unexampled, but very natural, for with a true instinct they feel and know that he is their greatest foe. Whether he means or wishes it, or no, he hurts them more than any million of men besides. He once said of them: "The Lords are up in a balloon;" elevated above the ordinary world, but unable to observe or affect the course of affairs. Another time he declared that he should think once, he should think twice, he should think three times before he would abolish the House of Lords; but if the third occasion passed, he did not say what his course would be. And these were the utterances of a man who had it in his power to fulfil his threats. More than once he has compelled the Lords to do his bidding by the menace of adding to their number or lessening their hereditary privileges. When they obstinately resisted the abolition of Purchase in the Army—although the measure had passed the House of Commons and was unmistakably approved by the nation—Gladstone revived a disused prerogative of the Crown, and forced the Queen to declare Purchase abolished by Royal Warrant—a weapon that had not been resorted to for two hundred years. He strained the Constitution, but he conquered the Lords. The last great difference between him and them was upon the extension of the franchise. In this instance the peers yielded in time; but had they held out, he would undoubtedly have shaken the very foundations of their position as legislators.

This single man who threatens and assails one of the ancient orders of the State, who places himself in antagonism with an entire aristocracy, who forces a still powerful class to abandon its privileges and trample on its prejudices, is of course the object of their profoundest antipathy. But not only the aristocracy themselves; all the mass of their followers, all the prejudiced Tories of the middle and lower class, above all those of the press or the literary sort—detest the name of Gladstone. To compensate—about two-thirds of the English nation adore him. No one in England in my time could evoke the enthusiasm that followed him.

All this is the magic of genius as well as the

might of will; it comes from the combination of intellect and character; the belief in his intention, the knowledge of his achievement, the sympathy with his effort, the magnetism of his presence and personality; the authority of a born leader of men.

Of his natural gifts, eloquence is perhaps the most easily recognized. His oratory is fiery and convincing by turns, but more often fascinating and persuading. His lucidity of speech, though he is neither terse nor often epigrammatic, is so wonderful that he is famous for the charm he flings about the most abstruse questions of finance. His long involved sentences never weary, are never obscure, and always lead up to some lofty sentiment that either excites the imagination or touches the heart.

Like most men of genius, he excites a personal fascination that is irresistible. His conversation is seductive in its interest. You cannot turn away from it. He holds you, like the Ancient Mariner, till he tells his tale. I was once asked to meet him at dinner, when there was no American Minister in England. It was at the house of Lord Halifax, one of his colleagues in the cabinet, who had corresponded with me the winter before while I had a room at the White House; and whose letters had been avowedly written for me to show to President Grant. At the date of the dinner the discussions of the Treaty of Washington were at their height, and there were grave doubts of the success of the negotiation. Lord Halifax asked me to meet Mr. Gladstone, so that I might convey his opinions direct to the President. The Prime Minister talked half an hour with me alone on the subject of the Treaty, and under the circumstances he naturally wished to impress me very fully with his ideas. I saw him, therefore, to unusual advantage, and was never more impressed with the power of a man to expound and illustrate and enforce his views by conversation. Afterward he continued the talk on other themes, and discussed the difference between the British and the American constitutions, the permanency of the systems and institutions of both countries, and was as brilliant and as fascinating as his reputation had led me to anticipate. I remember his saying that the American constitution was the most perfect ever written by man, which as a good Englishman he could admit; for the British pride themselves on the fact that their constitution is unwritten. But he thought Americans had a great advantage in elbow-room, as he called it; and that our institutions could not be said to have stood their severest test till the United States became as crowded as England is to-day.

On another occasion, some years later, he was good enough to ask me to breakfast. It was on the morning of a day when there was to be a great debate, which he was to lead; the result might decide the fate of a momentous measure, and either retain him in power or overthrow him. He had at table a party of ten, only two of them ladies, and one of these his daughter. Among the other guests were a distinguished divine; an ecclesiastical architect, or architectural ecclesiastic, I forget which; the Liberal son of a duke; a member of the House of Commons, and so on. We sat at breakfast an hour and a half, but not a word was said about politics, not a reference was made to the debate in the evening. The principal subject discussed was the revision of the New Testament, which had just been given to the world. The Prime Minister was extremely interested in this theme. He is learned in his Greek, as every one knows, and quoted the original text freely. He was entirely opposed to the revision, as a substitute for the older version, and offered to lay five pounds that it would never be authorized to be read in the churches. I was amused to hear him offer a wager, and on such a theme, and said so to his daughter. She told me she had never known him make a bet but once before, and that was that Disraeli would be a peer before himself.

This versatility of attention displayed at such a moment was characteristic of his genius. His information is various and his learning catholic as well as profound; his power to discuss the most different themes astounding. When he was for a while out of office, and nominally in retirement, the activity of his mind was incessant. He wrote pamphlets on the Vatican decrees, published whole volumes on Homer and the Youth of the World (*Juventus Mundi*); and debated artistic, antiquarian, ecclesiastical, and purely literary subjects in half the periodicals in England. He was a lay reader at morning prayer in the parish church at Hawarden, and a hewer of wood in the park immediately afterward; and he answered himself every post card that any one chose to send him. Finally, came his wonderful attack on the Tory foreign policy, which tumbled Lord Beaconsfield headlong from office and reputation, and indeed terminated his career.

Mr. Gladstone's position in regard to the American rebellion was one of the mistakes of his life. He has had the courage to admit the mistake, and the magnanimity to seek to atone for it. He thought that the right of secession was implied, if not admitted, in the American constitution, and like most Englishmen, he failed to see the reasons that would have made the admission of that right practically impossible, even if it had been logically tenable. Even after his famous apology to the American people—" Kin Beyond Sea "—I heard him declare that he still could not see that Jefferson Davis was wrong. This is what I should call the *doctrinaire* side of his mind, which disappears or is hidden completely in his practical contests in English politics. No man can put abstract notions more completely aside than he, or so envelop them in a cloud of explanatory comment as to make them invisible and innocuous whenever it is desirable for his purposes.

He is indeed a curious development of the English type; a strange out-growth from the Anglo-Saxon root. With his ardent religious faith apparently never disturbed in this age of scientific and intelligent unbelief; with his lofty Christian sentiment, carried, however, more often into foreign than domestic politics; with the extraordinary indirectness of his mind in some of its workings, as manifested in the Ewelme and Collier affairs—he is in many ways as un-English a representative as it is possible to imagine. Intellectually I have sometimes thought him more like an American or a Frenchman. His keen penetration, his logical acuteness, his abstract philosophy remind one almost of Emerson at times, while in profundity and power of generalization, he is not unlike Montesquieu. From one point of view the most transcendental and unpractical of statesmen; yet when he descends from the lofty heights where he evolves his theories of arbitration and religion and doing good to one's enemies—to the arena of actual, daily politics, no one is shrewder, more politic, more adroit; no one sees the situation more clearly, and—far more important and rarer quality—no one is readier to adapt himself to the situation that he perceives. No one knows how to hit harder or parry better, or understands more exactly the strategy of important crises, and the tactics of significant details. No one has carried great measures through greater difficulties; against the opposition not only of avowed enemies, but of loyal friends; against the influence of the Queen, the dislike of high society, the rooted prejudices often of the English people, the disapproval occasionally of the best and soberest minds.

Yet he marches on in a career of successive triumphs. He defeats the heir to one of the oldest dukedoms in his family borough; he forces his colleagues to the support of measures they detest; he compels the acquiescence of the court; he arouses and sometimes justifies, the wildest apprehensions of his enemies. He is at this moment the most important and imposing figure in English politics; the leader in the army of progress before the world; the champion of the people in a land where they still need one; the ally of a down-trodden sister country, to whom he holds out a hand to assist her to rise. High-minded and high-purposed; with his faults, like all who are human, but battling always against wrong or in favor of the weak, he is indeed the modern knight-errant, with even a Quixotic dash of romance in his temperament; but able to support as well as to attack, to defend as well as to destroy. This veteran of nearly seventy-seven, dashing against his enemies with the vigor of youth, leading the common people of England whom he has raised to a position and power they have never known till now; urging them to make the first use of that power to undo the wrongs of centuries in Ireland; offering to the men who have just dealt him the severest blow the justice that they claim—this man may not extort from the aristocrats of Europe the approbation he deserves, but Americans and democrats, believers in the people and friends of the people everywhere, cannot but recognize in him at once the noblest and greatest statesman of his time.

# CIVIC AND SOCIAL LONDON.

### Society in London.
By a Foreign Resident. 12mo, Paper, 25 cents.

### The World of London.
By COUNT PAUL VASILI. 12mo, Paper, 25 cents.

### The Queens of Society.
By GRACE and PHILIP WHARTON. Illustrated by Doyle and the Brothers Dalziel. 12mo, Cloth, $1 75.

This entertaining volume presents a gossiping biography of several of the celebrated women who have held a conspicuous place in society. Among the distinguished names are those of the Duchess of Marlborough, Lady Mary Wortley Montagu, Lady Morgan, Lady Caroline Lamb, Miss Landon (the unfortunate L. E. L.), Madame de Staël, Madame Roland, Madame Récamier, and others, both of England and France.

### The Wits and Beaux of Society.
By GRACE and PHILIP WHARTON. With Illustrations by H. B. GODWIN and JAMES GODWIN. 12mo, Cloth, $1 75.

This gossipy book gives sketches of such men as George Villiers, the second Duke of Buckingham, with numerous anecdotes of his adventures; the celebrated Grammont and Rochester, wherein the author introduces some incidents in the lives of such people as Hortense Mancini, the little Jermyn, La Belle Hamilton, and other noted beauties of France and England; Beau Nash; Lord Hervey; Scarron, and here, again, of his wife; and so on of numerous worthies or unworthies, each and all of whom are more or less known to fame.

### Wills's Old Leaves.
Old Leaves: Gathered from *Household Words*. By W. HENRY WILLS. 12mo, Cloth, $1 25.

It presents series of lively sketches of several of the prominent institutions of London, with frequent glimpses of the inferior social strata which serve as the basis of modern civilization.

---

PUBLISHED BY HARPER & BROTHERS, NEW YORK.

☞ *Any of the above works sent by mail, postage prepaid, to any part of the United States or Canada, on receipt of the price.*

# MEMOIR OF PRINCE ALBERT.

The Early Years of his Royal Highness the Prince Consort. Compiled, under the Direction of her Majesty the Queen, by Lieutenant-General the Honorable CHARLES GREY. Two Portraits. 12mo, Cloth, $1 00.

---

"In regard to the effect of the volume upon the people of England, should her Majesty hereafter resolve to publish it, there cannot, I think, be the shadow of a doubt, should it ever come before them, that it would exalt the loyalty and love of all true-hearted Englishmen. Where everything is so pure, so lovely, and so true, why should not our honored and beloved Queen lay open the innermost recesses of her heart, and thereby fix forever the loyal sympathy of all who have faith in what is good, and hold true Christian allegiance to their God and to their country?

"You will forgive me for noting down one or two thoughts which struck me while reading your volume. We now see, from first to last, the beautiful consistency of the Prince's character. He was a lovely boy with a gentle temper; yet even then he had a mental strength above his years, which gave him the mastery over his elder brother. And so it was in after-life. Those gentler qualities which made him the purest pattern of domestic love never for a moment degenerated into feebleness or effeminacy, but were carried out into a noble purpose by their unbroken union with the firm will of his great and unselfish heart. From his earliest years he seems never to have flinched from labor, and he had amassed vast treasures of exact knowledge, which he did not for a moment exhibit for ostentation, but he made them bear, at every turn of life, upon some intellectual aim or some plan that would tell upon the moral and physical good of his fellow-creatures."—Professor SEDGWICK, *Secretary to the Prince as Chancellor of the University of Cambridge.*

---

PUBLISHED BY HARPER & BROTHERS, NEW YORK.

☞ *The above work sent by mail, postage prepaid, to any part of the United States or Canada, on receipt of the price.*

# QUEEN VICTORIA'S JOURNAL.

**LEAVES FROM THE JOURNAL OF OUR LIFE IN THE HIGHLANDS, from 1848 to 1861.** To which are prefixed and added Extracts from the same Journal giving an Account of Earlier Visits to Scotland, and Tours in England and Ireland, and Yachting Excursions. Edited by Sir ARTHUR HELPS. 12mo, Cloth, $1 00.

**MORE LEAVES FROM THE JOURNAL OF A LIFE IN THE HIGHLANDS, from 1862 to 1882.** With Portrait. 4to, Paper, 15 cents. Pocket Edition, with Portraits, Illustrations, and Autographs. pp. 172. 16mo, Paper, 25 cents.

The book tells the story of the widowed life of a queen. It affords touching glimpses of a chilling isolation of personal position, which is none the less real because in the nature of things it must be rare. But it is its simple human interest that gives the book its strongest appeal. The reader rises from its perusal with the feeling that he has learned something more of the good woman by whom it was written—that above all else he has seen her in that hour of desolation which comes to many good women, and must be borne by all to whom it comes.—*N. Y. Mail and Express.*

Throughout the whole journal there is more of the woman than of the queen, and of simple human interest than of royal magnificence. It is safe to say that no queen of a great empire ever lived so much of the simple, natural life of a woman, and was so much absorbed in it as this Victoria I.—*Independent*, N. Y.

We have here almost everywhere the queen without her crown. Official state is laid aside as far as possible, and we see the mother, the friend, the sympathetic mourner with the sorrowing, the appreciative student of nature, and the interested tourist.—*Congregationalist*, Boston.

The interest of this little book is much increased by portraits and other illustrations. No one can read it without feeling the heart drawn out in sympathy with the illustrious writer. Its perfect naturalness, its almost childlike simplicity and open-heartedness, are very striking.—*Religious Herald*, Hartford.

---

PUBLISHED BY HARPER & BROTHERS, NEW YORK.

☛ *Either of the above works sent by mail, postage prepaid, to any part of the United States or Canada, on receipt of the price.*

# INTERESTING BIOGRAPHICAL WORKS.

### Fitzgerald's George the Fourth.
The Life of George the Fourth. Including his Letters and Opinions, with a View of the Men, Manners, and Politics of his Reign. By PERCY FITZGERALD. 12mo, Cloth, with Portraits, $2 00; in Two Parts, 4to, Paper, 40 cents.

### Mrs. Oliphant's The Queen. (Queen Victoria.)
The Queen. With 44 Engravings. 4to, Paper, 25 cents.

### Brougham's Autobiography.
The Life and Times of Henry, Lord Brougham. Written by Himself. 3 vols., 12mo, Cloth, in box, $6 00.

### Edward Bulwer, Lord Lytton.
Life, Letters, and Literary Remains of Edward Bulwer, Lord Lytton. By his Son, the EARL OF LYTTON ("Owen Meredith"). One Volume (containing Vols. I. and II. of the English Edition). Illustrated by Six Portraits, Eleven Wood-engravings, and Six Fac-similes of MSS., &c. Pages xx., 664. 12mo, Cloth, $2 75. 4to, Paper, in Two Parts, 20 cents each.

### Sydney Smith's Life and Times.
A Sketch of the Life and Times of the Rev. Sydney Smith (M.A., Rector of Combe-Florey, and Canon Residentiary of St. Paul's). Based on Family Documents and the Recollections of Personal Friends. By STUART J. REID. With Steel-plate Portraits, Numerous Illustrations, and Autograph Letter. 8vo, Cloth, $3 00.

### Trollope's Autobiography.
Autobiography of Anthony Trollope. With a Portrait. 12mo, Cloth, $1 25; 4to, Paper, 20 cents.

## Yates's Memoirs of a Man of the World.
Fifty Years of London Life. By EDMUND YATES. With Portrait. 12mo, Cloth, $1 75; also in Two Vols., 4to, Paper, 20 cents per volume.

## Forbes's Chinese Gordon.
Chinese Gordon. A Succinct Account of his Life. By ARCHIBALD FORBES. With Illustrations and a Map. 4to, Paper, 20 cents.

## Curran and his Contemporaries.
Curran and his Contemporaries. By CHARLES PHILLIPS. 12mo, Cloth, $1 50.

## Life of Lord Beaconsfield.
The Life of the Right Hon. Benjamin Disraeli, Earl of Beaconsfield, K.G. With Two Portraits. 4to, Paper, 10 cents.

## Lord Beaconsfield.
Lord Beaconsfield. A Study. By GEORG BRANDES. 4to, Paper, 15 cents.

## Beaconsfield's Home Letters.
Home Letters. By the late Earl of Beaconsfield. Illustrated. 12mo, Paper, 25 cents.

## Beaconsfield's Letters to his Sister.
Lord Beaconsfield's Correspondence with his Sister. 1832–1852. 12mo, Paper, 25 cents.

## Lucy's Gladstone.
William E. Gladstone. By H. W. LUCY. 32mo, Paper, 20 cents; Cloth, 35 cents.

---

PUBLISHED BY HARPER & BROTHERS, NEW YORK.

☞ *Any of the foregoing works sent by mail, postage prepaid, to any part of the United States or Canada, on receipt of the price.*

# JUSTIN McCARTHY'S HISTORIES.

## History of Our Own Times.

A History of Our Own Times, from the Accession of Queen Victoria to the General Election of 1880. By JUSTIN MCCARTHY, M.P. In Two Volumes. 4to, Paper, 20 cents each; 12mo, Cloth, $1 25 each; Half Calf, $3 00 each.

Will unquestionably maintain a high place in literature. It is scarcely an anticipation of the universal verdict on these pages to describe it as a rare achievement of literary workmanship.—*Daily News*, London.

## Short History of Our Own Times.

A Short History of Our Own Times, from the Accession of Queen Victoria to the General Election of 1880. By JUSTIN MCCARTHY, M.P. 4to, Paper, 25 cents; 12mo, Cloth, $1 50.

McCarthy's histories are even more charming than his fiction.—*N. Y. World*.

Brilliant without being flashy, easy without being careless, and accurate without being dry. As readable as a novel, and probably more read than most of the romances of the day.—*Daily News*, London.

## History of the Four Georges.

A History of the Four Georges. By JUSTIN MCCARTHY, M.P. Vol. I. 12mo, Cloth, $1 25. (To be completed in Four Volumes.)

Bids fair to be one of the most delightful and popular of Mr. McCarthy's works.—*N. Y. Telegram*.

Mr. McCarthy's new historical work exhibits the excellent qualities which won popularity for his "History of Our Own Times." His narrative is clear, easy, and rapid. His personages are alive.—*N. Y. Tribune*.

---

PUBLISHED BY HARPER & BROTHERS, NEW YORK.

☞ *Any of the above works sent by mail, postage prepaid, to any part of the United States or Canada, on receipt of the price.*

www.ingramcontent.com/pod-product-compliance
Lightning Source LLC
Chambersburg PA
CBHW030809230426
43667CB00008B/1137